INTENTIONAL LIVING

*finding the inner peace to create
successful relationships*

by
Dr. Barbara Stroud

ISBN: 150071836X
ISBN 13: 9781500718367
Library of Congress Control Number: 2014914311
CreateSpace Independent Publishing Platform
North Charleston, South Carolina

DEDICATION

Intentional Living is about the power of relationships. This text is dedicated to a relationship that has served me throughout my lifetime—a relationship that has encouraged me, fed my soul, and pushed me to do great things. Strong relationships seed powerful individuals, and with that in mind, I dedicate this book to my mother, Patricia.

DEDICATION

ACKNOWLEDGMENTS

Writing *Intentional Living* was a journey of self-understanding for me, and I hope this is true for the reader as well. However, such a grand process of change and self-discovery is rarely completed without the support of others. The completion of this text would not have happened without the guidance and unfailing support of my writing team.

First, to my editor and reflective support, Esther Chon, who walked this journey with me; her meaningful insights have strengthened both me and the overall quality of the text. Carolyn Wingfield acted as the primary research assistant, providing validation of the science presented throughout. Finally, a list of strong readers who provided reviews and helpful feedback to increase the accessibility of the text: Jennifer Black, Karen Olivares, Saroja Raman, Kanchana Tate, and Laura Westland. Relationships sustain us, direct us, and hold us in times of need and growth.

TABLE OF CONTENTS

CHAPTER 1

Introduction

There is great power in the brain as well as in the history and knowledge about you held by your brain. However, most of us do not know how to make use of this brain power to better understand ourselves in relationship. Many of us go through life repeating the same relationship mistakes, wanting to be different but not knowing how. This book takes you to a deeper understanding of your own brain from a practical point of view. Everyone can relate to the ideas and experiences presented here. The overall goal is to help you harness the power of your own brain to build self-understanding and create positive personal change, thereby living intentionally.

To fully live in an intentional manner, with power and control over your choices and emotional health, you must understand the larger functions and goals of the brain. *Intentional Living* is related to living a life that is purposeful, focused, and self-determined.

- Do not let past relationships guide your future behavior.
- Begin by learning to let go of painful past emotional messages that are not productive in your current life circumstances.
- Build the skills to respond more proactively to stressors in your daily life.

- The uniqueness of your individual experience, family culture, and personal views is also taken into account in this journey toward self-improvement. Knowing yourself and understanding your brain's power will lead to personal growth.
- We all can improve, grow in our relationships, and overcome past hurt when we seek to do so from an *intentional* perspective.

To support your understanding, I discuss the brain in two constructs, which support thinking and feelings. The complexity of the brain informs us that our emotional experience is held in multiple regions of the brain, working in concert with the thinking aspects of the brain. Thus, the brain does not act in separate and distinct mechanisms but as a united whole. I delineate the two functional aspects here to enhance your self-knowledge and help you harness your personal potential.

The content of this book is largely informed by current neuroscience. I have been honored to gain knowledge in the presence of current leaders in the field, such as Ed Tronick, Peter Fonagy, Bruce Perry, Connie Lillas, and Daniel Siegel. My thinking is informed by their work and yet is uniquely different. I have deliberately sought to use the current brain science and translate this knowledge into everyday language. Science is often held in the universities and research volumes. I wanted this important and life-changing science to be available for anyone and everyone. In a very practical and day-to-day manner, the text takes you through a deeper understanding of the emotional and thinking functions of the brain. Next, I work to help you understand your role in shaping past messages and future choices to promote healthier relationships. My larger goal with this text is to help you help yourself live better, love honestly, and become free from the emotional pain of the past.

Happy reading. Life is a journey; much like a roller coaster, there are ups and downs. My hope is that the ups outweigh the downs.

CHAPTER 2

Your Brain as the CEO
of Your Experiences

The brain serves multiple functions in the activities of living. This book will directly address how your brain influences your emotional world (your emotional world can be defined as the feelings you assign to life events—past, present, and future) and your relationships with others. Your brain is the executive officer that manages your experiences. I hope to help you learn how to partner with this CEO to improve your quality of life. Understanding the brain is paramount to self-understanding as related to relationships (social interactions) and successful communication (being heard and hearing others). How does the brain direct our social interactions or your interpersonal world? Your interpersonal world relates to how you build internal understanding of social experiences and interpersonal relationships.

To better understand the brain, you must understand what it does. I will focus on three primary functions of the brain in order to increase your deeper understanding of your interpersonal world (these are by no means the only significant activities of the brain). To support self-understanding, you must explore the brain's role in life and brain-involved events such as relationship history, understanding feelings, and stress responses. These three areas of focus will first be outlined briefly here and then explored in more depth later in this chapter.

a. Relationship History:
- Our brains hold unconscious or inaccessible memories of relationships from the past. These memories (verbal and nonverbal) shape our current relationship experience and the internal understanding of relationships that we create and hold in our minds. Consider your beliefs and values about interpersonal relationships. These ideas or beliefs live in the warehouse of your mind, waiting to be called into action in your next interpersonal exchange.

b. Understanding Feelings:
- The brain controls emotional experiences. Our brains, as influenced by our experiences with significant others, define for us what feelings mean, how to express them, and what they say about us and the people in our lives. In fact, there are areas of our brains fully dedicated to the expression of emotion, the modulation of feelings, and the storage of emotional memories.[1]

c. Stress Responses:
- Our brains also modulate or organize our stress-response systems. The stress-response system refers to the manner in which your body and mind have learned over time (from past experiences) to react to stressful or emotionally challenging life events. Stress responses are trained very early in life. These responses, through repetition and intensity of occurrence, grow to become automatic.[2] When an event sets off the stress-response system, the brain can behave in one of three ways, as seen in the Stress Response Chart on the next page.

Stress Response Chart

(The below chart is adapted from the work of Lillas and Turnbull)[3]

Stress Response Patterns	What Others Might See	What You Might Feel
Excited or agitated response	Fight or flight, alertness, combative or argumentative, high emotional response	Emotionally overwhelmed, increase in heart rate, shortness of breath, irrational thinking
Shut-down or disconnected response	Disengagement from the event, listlessness, sadness, lack of involvement, ignoring the issue, denial of a concern, low emotional investment in the events	Numb, apathetic, disinterested, ineffective, tired
Mixed-pattern response	Panic and being frozen, anxiety, worry, or no outward response may be evident	Panic, anxiety, trapped, out of control, fearful, wanting to avoid

In the section below, I will examine the concepts of relationship history, emotional understanding, and stress responses in greater detail. You should note that as we move through the text, we will return to these pivotal brain functions.

Relationship History

Healthy relationships allow individuals to realistically measure past experiences against current interpersonal events. Your brain functions as the recorder or secretary, if you will, of past events; it holds memories (accessible and inaccessible) and stores these memories for later use. These memories are not always known to your conscious mind. Many of these interpersonal-relationship-based memories can be experienced more as feelings than ideas. Consider your childhood home during the winter holidays. The holiday season often brings about many smells that are associated with the occasion. Can you recall a smell that was common in your home when you were a child (pine, tamales, turkey, bean paste soup, or collard greens)? When you consider these smells even now, your mind takes you back to early memories. As you explore the various events that come to mind, you may find yourself recalling the feelings related to those events more than the details of what occurred. Emotion and memory are highly linked,[4] and we often remember a feeling before an event. Strong memories can create fear, shame, hopelessness, or anger, and these intense feelings may be related more to a memory than to what's going on in the present. Have you ever found yourself becoming very angry over a small thing (the straw that breaks the camel's back)? Well, these strong emotions that seem irrational may remind you of a similar event that was painful, overwhelming, or did not resolve positively. Or, as the "camel's back" reference implies, your seemingly irrational feelings may be the result of an accumulation of similar events stored over time in the memory centers of your brain, and this one event initiates a response based on a laundry list of similar and perhaps negative experiences.

Now as an example, let's consider Sally as she waits for Nancy to join her for lunch. At ten minutes past the appointed meeting time, Sally begins to worry and starts feeling restless. After twenty minutes, she becomes agitated and wonders what is wrong with Nancy, thinking, "She knows I hate to wait, and she has never been late before." Sally's anger at Nancy continues. "Nancy could have called. How selfish of her. She does not care how I feel. What an insensitive thing to do, leaving me here waiting for her." Sally's anger increases, and she walks out of the restaurant highly agitated (in a full stress response), telling herself, "I thought Nancy was a true friend, but just as I thought, you cannot trust anyone to keep their promises. Well, I guess I do not need that friend." Later that night, Nancy calls Sally to tell her how sorry she was for missing lunch. Nancy had been at the police department reporting her purse stolen. All her contact information was in her cell phone, which had been in the stolen purse. Nancy continues, saying that when she got home, she fell asleep. Immediately upon waking up, Nancy called Sally. She says, "I hated to keep you waiting—I know that you are always on time and I work to be timely as well."

Past relationships play an important role in this example. Sally's reaction to Nancy being late was more about her relationship history than about Nancy's behavior. Sally grew up with an alcoholic father. He was often late, and he disappointed her on many occasions. Sally's father would forget her birthday and show up late for dinner; he arrived drunk to her high school graduation. Sally has strong personal memories of waiting for her father to take her to special events and him never showing up. This relationship history of abandonment, disappointment, and feeling devalued is held in Sally's brain. Thus similar events that involve disappointment can initiate those same feeling, even though the person or the events are very different. Memories of past relationships can shape current and future relationships.

Adults learn to be in relationships (or learn the social ways of being in the world) by participating in social interactions within their families as young children. Who taught you to say please and thank you, and not to scratch your behind in public? Who taught you the quality and tone of emotional expression? You learned these social skills by experiencing them in a relationship, not by reading a book or taking a class. If you come from a family system where people talk loudly and openly share their emotions, then this is your experience of normal emotional communication. If your partner grew up in a family where there was little open communication of emotions and loud voices led to yelling and fighting, your partner may ask, "Why is your family always yelling and angry?" It is not the activity of yelling that gives the impression of anger but the history and memory of yelling (the meaning of yelling in your partner's family culture) and past experiences that lead your partner to this assumption. The brain holds our past experiences,[5] and like it or not, our history is always a part of us. So awareness of how your brain processes relationships and social experiences is a big part of intentional living. Once emotion is stirring in a present relationship, the self-examining question becomes: "Is my brain responding to this moment or an emotional memory from a past relationship?" This information is coupled with your active use of choice to determine your actions at the moment of emotional challenge. To build intentional living skills, you must build an understanding of your own relationship history, pay attention to those memories (even the unspoken ones), and seek to gain control of that which has been controlling you. The questions we must explore to be more intentional in our relationships with others are: "Can I train my brain to support my ability to understand a new relationship as separate and distinct from my past relationships?" and "Can I act and build true feelings around the current set of relationship experiences based on the current unique circumstance, unencumbered by my relationship history—the proverbial 'old baggage'?"

Let's look at Sally's example of "old baggage" impacting her current relationships. Sally is waiting for Nancy, who is late for a lunch date. The experience of waiting for Nancy initiates historical feelings from Sally's past relationship with her father. The emotions Sally experiences are related to her past, as activated by current events. Sally's relationship with her father could be classified as an intense relationship, or highly significant life relationship, making the associated emotional memories quite strong.

The significance or strength of a relationship bond impacts how influential that relationship remains. For example, we often put greater importance on what is said to us by friends or family than by acquaintances or passing strangers. Sally was kept waiting by her father not once but multiple times, which created a pattern of being disappointed and forgotten, such that this became the rule and not the exception. So how does Sally begin to live more intentionally, not allowing her past to drive her future?

Sally must recognize that her emotional experience is more about the past than the present. She needs to ponder her relationship past, understanding it as an important part of her life history. However, she does not have to let past relationships dictate current behavior. Her emotions are strong and belong to her experience with her father. The anger, sadness, and hurt she feels is not about Nancy but about what this event reminds Sally of from her past, as held within the resources of her relationship memory banks. This intentional living activity will not make Sally's negative feelings go away, but it will help Sally not to blame Nancy for her strong emotional response to the current set of events. Sally's anger, sadness, and disappointment were a real part of her relationship history. However, this history does not define Sally unless she carries these strong feelings into each new relationship.

Throughout this text, I will provide personal development activities to assist you in making use of the provided information in real-world experiences from your personal life. The following personal development activity has been designed to help create a deeper understanding of relationships as well as the influences of relationship history.

Personal Development Activity

Building Relationships Understanding		
List 5 qualities you look for in a good friend	1._____ 2._____ 3._____ 4._____ 5._____	*Examples:* *Honesty* *Caring* *Humor* *Acceptance*
List 5 qualities you recently found present in a friend that led to ending the relationship	1._____ 2._____ 3._____ 4._____ 5._____	*Examples:* *Selfishness* *Dishonesty* *Insensitivity* *Uncontrolled anger*
Define 5 things you bring to a relationship that make you a good friend	1._____ 2._____ 3._____ 4._____ 5._____	*Examples:* *Kindness* *Patience* *Sensitivity* *Understanding* *Honesty*
List 3 to 5 events that remind you of a negative relationship history event	1._____ 2._____ 3._____ 4._____ 5._____	*Examples:* *When others yell* *Feeling embarrassed* *When people laugh at my accent*

Understanding Feelings

Understanding your feelings is a major key to intentional living. When you are able to understand your feelings, they do not necessarily drive your behavior. Rather, feelings help to describe your behavior and the emotional experience brought on by current events. There are moments when your emotional experience becomes so strong that you cannot access your thinking brain. Discussed in chapter 5, this experience is highly related to your stress-response system. In optimal circumstances, you are able to balance both the thinking and emotional qualities of the brain in order to enhance emotional understanding, thus allowing for intentional decision making. Optimal circumstances are often created when you feel emotionally safe within the framework of a trusting and nurturing relationship.

Intentional living is about knowing what you feel and knowing why you feel it. From this point, you can make an intentional (informed) decision about what to do next, thus not only taking ownership of your feelings but also choosing what to do with them. Once you can name the feeling, it need not have power over you. Remember, your feelings are your responsibility, even when they are stimulated by the activities of another (your partner, coworker, child, or fellow driver). Understanding your feelings is the beginning of self-understanding.

To better comprehend your feelings, you also have to understand the physiological indicators of your emotional experience. It is true that emotions happen to us and lead to a physiological[6] response. The labeling of this physiological event is shaped over time by experiences in relationship, cultural norms, and repetition. So the meaning of "sadness" is a culmination of physical experience, the culturally based or family-led defining of that experience, and repeated opportunities to have the same feeling coupled with the same label (sadness) over time. The body's internal physical response becomes paired with the emotional understanding, and sadness now has a meaning that is alive in a family and cultural context.

Your body experiences events in different ways. How you experience people and events is held in your sensory system. This is the part of your body and brain that organizes sensations from the external world into a meaningful whole that can be used by the body and brain.[7] Here is a sensory example: you smell something cooking in the kitchen; you feel the heat as you pass the oven; you open the door and you see the golden brown chunks sinking into shape as the balls of raw dough melt into firm cookies. Your brain pulls all this information together and says, "Oh, someone is making cookies." The same is true of feelings—you have a set of body responses that indicate fear, joy, excitement, or distress, and your brain pulls together all the available sensory information to create a definition of the events in place. The next personal development activity is designed to help you understand what physical sensations are related to specific emotional states.

Personal Development Activity

Understanding Feelings					
Self-examination questions	How did it feel in your body?	What was the rhythm of your heart?	What were the tone and pace of your voice?	Did you feel your breathing change? If so, how?	What did you do? How did you treat others?
Think of the last time you were in a state of joy or excitement.					
Think of the last time you were in a state of fear or anxiety.					
Think of the last time you were in a state of anger or blind rage.					
Think of the last time you were in a state of relaxation and emotional calm.					

Stress Responses

Stressful life events impact your brain, body, and emotions. Human beings are biologically driven to respond to stress in order to survive. The first function of your stress-response system is to keep you safe and alive.[8] Stress ignites hormonal activity in the brain. Stress hormones in small amounts are helpful. For example, a small amount of stress hormones before public speaking, a driving test, or a sporting event can improve your performance. However, in large doses, and without strategies of stress recovery, stress hormones can be unproductive, and even harmful.

Whether we are threatened by a lion or facing test anxiety, the same stress hormones are discharged into our systems. We prescribe different interpretations depending on the context of specific events: the stress of a test vs. the stress of a job interview vs. the stress of police lights flashing behind you while you drive. There are specific events that create stress for the majority of people, such as job interviews, tests, nightshift work, lack of sleep, etc. Then there are individual stressors, which are more specific or unique to each of us. Sometimes we refer to these as our "buttons" or "pet peeves." I will refer to such personal stressors as "emotional triggers." Your personal interpretation, or the level of risk you attribute to the events, feeds the magnitude of your stress response. Once your stress response is engaged, your sensory system launches into a physiological response of sensations that signal stress alert telling the body to protect itself and survive.

Because a stress response ignites the emotional centers of the brain and decreases your capacity for logical thinking, greater self-understanding about your stress response will be helpful. Becoming aware of the emotional triggers (events, words, people, and situations) that produce stress or extreme emotional distress for you is an important step toward intentional living. Having a goal of knowing your individual emotional triggers helps you to focus on the triggering event—not the emotional content, the person or people involved, or their responses (appropriate or inappropriate) to the event.

One way to help yourself understand your emotional triggers is to pay attention to the events, environments, or people that have led you to experience one of the three stress responses. The three stress response styles include excited, shut-down, and mixed-pattern responses. As an example, imagine your alarm does not go off and you are now late for work or school. An excited response would be to jump up, heart racing, and prepare to leave the house while panicking. A shut-down response would be to cover your head with the blankets, saying something like, "Well, I am already late—why bother?" and then going back to sleep. A mixed pattern would involve the internal debate of whether to get up or stay in bed, with no clear action taken in either direction. One thing to note here is that each person has different stress responses to different events or experiences. No one person always has an excited response or a shut-down response. When you stop to examine your stress-response style, you will find that it shifts with events, the availability of emotionally supportive others, and your access to internal resources.

Imagine you have been called into your boss's office to discuss a workflow issue. Someone on the team has dropped the ball, and it is now your responsibility to fix the problem—and quickly. Your employer is very upset—yelling, pointing, and threatening that someone will pay. This is one of the company's largest accounts, and the deadline is in three days. Now everything is riding on you, and your stress-response system is in full gear. Once your stress-response system is activated, you may find yourself experiencing some of the emotions mentioned in the stress response chart presented earlier. When you are having an excited response, you may feel your heart racing, experience a lack of mental clarity, and have a flood of ideas and emotions. Thoughts associated with this pattern could include: "How can I get this done myself? So much to do—so little time." A matrix of each stress-response style along with some of the thoughts and feelings that might go with each style of response is presented on the next page.

Possible Stress Response Reactions for the Current Example

Stress Response	Feelings	Thoughts
Excited	Overwhelmed, unfocused,	Now it is all up to me, and I have to get it right. The future of the company is on me.
Shut Down	Apathetic, numb	This is not my problem, and I could care less what happens to this company
Mixed	Fearful, lack of control	What if I screw this up? Now all eyes are on me and I have to deliver, but what if I cannot do it?

When you are stressed or emotionally overwhelmed, do you find yourself feeling angry, frustrated, depressed, emotionally numb, worried, or anxious?

Once you find yourself engulfed in the emotions of a stress response, your focus often turns to your emotional experience—not to the situation at hand. In other words, your stress-response system has now engaged the emotional center of your brain. Your response to the situation is overshadowed by your emotions, and you may respond more to the emotions than to the content of the event.

For instance, consider if you were to quit in the above example. Quitting your job might end the immediate stress response, but it would bring on a host of other problems. Moreover, quitting does not resolve the original cause of your stress response. Your agency still requires the completion of a major project. It is not uncommon to discover that when you act from a place of high emotional energy, you are often not thinking from a rational place and may make hasty and unwise decisions. Some of the best examples of irrational communication come from verbal disagreements with an intimate partner. Consider the last time you had an emotionally intense disagreement with a lover. Was anything said that you later regretted? If you did, this is a result of your stress response acting without your ability to filter thoughts or ideas.

Intentional living requires a conscious understanding of your stress-response style and the stress-response styles of significant others in your life (family, coworkers, your partner, and friends). When you know what you are feeling—although you may not be able to fully control it—you gain a deeper self-understanding along with power over your internal experience. This level of understanding can inform your choices, including your behavior toward yourself and others.

In the work example used earlier, your *emotional brain* (defined in more detail in chapter 4) may say something like, "This is so unfair. I did not make this mess, and I get stuck cleaning it all up." Meanwhile, your *thinking brain* (which is outlined in the next chapter) can focus on a larger goal, such as, "What is best for the company is good for me, and if I can fix this issue, it will only increase my value at the company." Once your stress indicator engages, it becomes challenging to be in relationships, create social success, and learn and adapt to life changes. Stress is not a friend to relationship success, professional achievement, positive parenting choices, or competent decision making. You can learn to intentionally manage the stress in your life and not let stress control you.

The Uniqueness of You

The problem with many self-help books is that they offer a one-size-fits-all approach to personal problems. Individual differences cannot be ignored in the explanation of relationships and social behavior. The areas we have discussed previously in this chapter—relationship history, understanding emotions, and stress response—take a unique trajectory for each individual reader. As an author, I hope to make it clear that the value you find in this book will be determined by how you apply the concepts to yourself, your individual relationships, your family, your cultural understanding, and your personal interpretation of your emotional experiences. No book or therapist can tell you who you are or what you can become. It is up to you to discover your potential. As an author and a psychologist, I simply want to point out some steps that can help you reach your optimal potential.

Culture is an important part of the human experience, which means it plays a role in understanding the self and the self in relationship. As a starting place, understand that culture is greater than race or ethnicity. While these elements influence culture, there is much more involved. Culture is often defined as the values or beliefs individuals hold sacred and allow to shape their behavior.[9] You behave in a certain manner because you stand on a value that indicates this is the proper way to act. These underlying beliefs may be shared by a group. For example, your ethnicity, your religion, your profession, or your generation may share views or values similar to your own. Just as your personal values and cultural self-understanding are sacred to you, the person next to you holds values and a cultural self-understanding that are equally sacred to them, whether they are from the same culture as you or a different one.

How does this relate to intentional living? Often we wish to describe individuals with different cultural beliefs as "wrong" or "bad." Remember intentional living is about gaining self-knowledge to guide your behavior in relationships. Perhaps in your culture or self-understanding, breastfeeding is a private activity, reserved for the home. If this is your value, a woman breastfeeding in public goes against your deeply held beliefs. Seeing her breastfeeding may upset you and send your stress-response system into activation. Rather than acting on your stress response and perhaps scolding the breastfeeding mother, you can respond intentionally by accepting that, while you may not like or agree with this mother's practice, she holds a strong set of personal values that guide her decision. Her value to breastfeed in public is just as salient, sacred, and deeply personal as your value against the same practice. Intentional living embraces the value of not judging others. While holding on to your strong beliefs, you learn to accept that others can possess different ideals.

You are asked at this point to consider culture from two perspectives: culture "from the inside out" and culture "from the outside in." Culture from the inside out is your internalized, personal view of who you are along with the way you see yourself as influenced by multiple factors or diversity issues that encompass your culture, or self-knowing. Culture from the outside in involves the external, stereotyped prejudgments that others assign to you. The self-determining question is: Will you allow outside-in factors to define you, or will you hold true to your inside-out definition of who you choose to be?

Intentional living holds cultural values as significant to all understanding about the self and the other. We must know, individually, what we believe and hold dear—that which represents a point of no return in our personal worlds, such as an idea or value that is unchanging.

Step one is to know yourself. *What do I hold as true? What do I believe in? Where can I be flexible and where are my values unchanging?*

Step two is to know your emotional trigger point. This refers to a behavior that sets off an attack on your values and engages your stress response. An example might be seeing a women breastfeeding when that activity is in conflict with your beliefs. It is at this point that your stress response has kicked in. What do you do next?

Step three is to take action. Is this a circumstance in which you should defend your value for the safety of yourself and others? Or is this an experience in which you can choose to disagree and take the   higher road, knowing you do not have to change the other person and that you lose nothing by holding to your beliefs in silence. Just as you have an inside-out cultural self-knowledge, so too does the person whom you are judging from an outside-in cultural lens.

The upcoming personal development activity has been designed to help you identify step one in the process of understanding personal values and strong beliefs. When you consider the ideals stated in the left-hand column of the chart, can you indicate your belief as related to these issues? Are there acceptable variations of these practices, ones which will not compromise your beliefs or set off your stress response? The final column asks you to point out the variations of the ideals that you personally cannot accept. At this level of the practice, consider now how you might wish to respond in such a situation. Considering your options while you are calm may prepare you for when you are faced with a highly inflammatory cultural conflict.

Personal Development Activity

Personal Values Explored			
Value-based activity	**What I believe**	**What I will accept**	**What I cannot tolerate**
Ex: *Breastfeeding*	*Private activity for home only*	*Other women have different practices*	*Women that do not feel the need to cover their breasts in public*
Public displays of affection			
Interracial marriage			
Including prayer in schools			
Legalizing marijuana			
Gay rights			
Add your idea			
Add your idea			

Remember, cultural values are highly connected to emotional understanding, and when our values become challenged, an emotional trigger often results.

In summary, we have used this chapter to outline the seminal issues that will frame our ongoing discussions around issues of intentional living. Your relationship history, emotional understanding, stress-response style, and personal culture are all elements that will continue to be examined across this text. To support your self-awareness, we will continue introducing personal development activities. Your process of knowing your brain, as influenced by your history, has just begun; there is much to discover together.

CHAPTER 3

The Thinking Brain

As we continue to explore intentional living and purposeful behavior, it is important to understand the thinking and feeling functions of the brain; this next section will discuss the thinking elements. The brain supports multiple activities related to living, including but not limited to heart rate, breathing, vision, hearing, movement, memory, attention, learning, emotions, and cognition.[1] As we examine the brain's thinking elements, we will look at the activities attributed to your thinking brain. We will also consider the question of how your thinking brain influences daily living. Next we will examine how your thinking brain is actively involved in relationships including how it helps shape the understanding of your relationship history and your emotional self-knowledge. Finally, we will examine your thinking brain's role in intentional living.

The Thinking Brain

Human beings have the neurological capacity for advanced reasoning, hypothetical extrapolation, creative expansion, analysis, and interpretation. We spend a great deal of our time thinking or engaged in cognitive activities, such as analyzing, reasoning, remembering, organizing, and using logic. Your thinking brain is responsible for cognitive or analytic tasks. Examples include preparing a meal, creating a shopping list, and designing the quickest route home from work—all types of planning. Another thinking task is that of decision making. You wake in the morning, get out of bed, and then make a choice: "Will I brush my teeth first, or take a shower?" This is a cognitive (or thinking brain task). "What should I wear today?" Again, you are making a decision, or thinking. What to have for breakfast is yet another daily choice. These are all functions of your thinking brain. Your thinking brain is at work all day, every day. Yet we are not even aware of how often we are engaged in cognitive tasks. Consider the cognitive activities of your daily routine. Several times in a day, you are organizing tasks (*What should I do first?*), considering consequences (*If I take this exit, will I get home faster?*), calculating (*The 13-ounce sale bag of chips is cheaper than the 10-ounce regular-price bag of chips*), or finding solutions (*If we are out of sour cream, I should be able to use plain yogurt in this recipe*).[2]

Thinking is an important and necessary life skill. Our very survival depends on the ability to think, make good decisions, consider outcomes, and select the best option available. In the United States, our academic institutions are highly focused on cognitive skills and building thinking abilities. This is a positive direction, as strong thinking skills are necessary in the workforce—to support new business development, create innovative products, and fuel the economy.

Consider students at any stage: elementary school, high school, or college. All of their academic tasks in English, history, science, math, etc., involve their thinking brains. "What about art or music?" some readers might ask. While these artistic and expressive endeavors do focus more on process than product, the teaching and learning of art and music involves the activity of thinking. In art, you consider color composition, the structure of a sculpture. Music is filled with elements of math (counting quarter, half, and whole notes) and reading another language (reading music is a decoding skill that involves thinking). Strong thinking skills lead to success in school. In short, our academic goals should be to train good thinkers.

On a different note, consider your workplace. Your thinking brain should be fully activated in order to produce a quality work performance and support productive outcomes. Activities such as responding to e-mail, creating an invoice, developing project proposals, estimating time to complete a task, budgeting, designing workflows, and evaluating final products all involve thinking. What would your day be like without thinking? Consider the cognitive skills you use most at work.

The activities of cooking, managing household finances, and even planning a vacation all involve the thinking brain. Now consider the cognitive skills you use at home. I suggest that you do not go a day without thinking, and your thinking brain is a powerful tool that can improve your life when used intentionally.

How the Thinking Brain Influences Your Relationships

If your thinking brain is involved in the cognitive tasks of learning, working, and planning, how does this relate to the skills of intentional living? How we think about a relationship or a person influences how we behave in our relationship with that person. Building self-awareness around the activities of your thinking brain as related to interpersonal experiences shapes your ability to be more intentional in your response to others.

Your thinking brain is actively involved in interpersonal activities or social relationships that together make up your interpersonal world.[3] Being in relationship involves thinking, planning, hypothesizing, using judgment, and interpreting. These are all thinking brain activities. When we meet a friend for lunch, we plan where and when to dine. We often hypothesize what others are thinking and use our judgment regarding how much personal information to share with someone else. We are constantly interpreting the verbal and nonverbal feedback we receive and altering our responses in accordance to our internal judgments. All of this thinking happens in the moment, often without our awareness. When you think about any relationship that influences your life, you are thinking or evaluating that person. For instance, when I think about my partner, I may consider the attributes I enjoy as well as the things I wish to change. I am simultaneously creating a way to understand the other person in the relationship and engaging in an interactive social experience with the other person. In other words, you are constantly assessing the relationship while remaining actively involved in the relationship experience.

For a personal example, select a person in your life with whom you spend a great deal of time—a coworker, a best friend, or a family member. How would you describe this person? What are the traits you enjoy or find positive about this person? These are the thoughts or ideas you associate with that relationship. You have thoughts and feelings (feelings live in your emotional brain—chapter 4) associated with each of your friends, family members, and acquaintances. These ideas, thoughts, and feelings you hold in your mind about the other person become your way of understanding the relationship. If a relationship came with a set of instructions, the ideas your mind creates becomes the instruction booklet. The set of instructions for, or the relational way of, being with your parent is different than the rule of engagement with a friend or a coworker.

Now consider someone you do not know well—your favorite celebrity, a stranger next to you on the bus, the clerk at the grocery store. You do not know this person, but you could offer a description. Additionally, you might take some facts about this person and begin to "fill in the blanks," taking educated guesses about the individual's personal style or interpersonal traits. This is your thinking brain at work in the relationship. Your brain is working to create a mental picture that defines the person you only know casually or not at all. You are building a set of instructions to go with this less familiar relationship. Your brain has a small amount of data, and you fill in the blanks to create a full story. Your thinking brain does this often, without your conscious awareness, and you hold ideas and assumptions about people you do not know.

We engage in creating a story, or rules, for those we do not know well. Sometimes, larger societal norms or personality stereotypes influence the labels we create for others. For example, societal cultural myths state that artists are overly emotional, blondes are not very smart, and engineers lack social skills. Our brains, at times, fill in missing data with universal and culturally influenced stereotypes (those emerging from outside-in culture). It is not a bad activity—just a way your thinking brain organizes information. The danger would be to act on these assumptions only to discover you were wrong. The ways our thinking brains work to define the people in our lives make up our relational world and interpersonal experience.

Relationship History and The Thinking Brain

Your thinking brain is highly involved in the way you describe and understand past relationships. Recall, from chapter 2, the importance of relationship history in intentional living. Not only does the thinking brain label and organize current relationships but it also holds a descriptive understanding of past relationships. For example, an individual with a relationship history of an abusive sibling may take that history into other experiences with people who bring to mind the abusive brother or sister. Similarly, a person with a history of a generous, caring, and unselfish sibling may expect others who seem, in ways, similar to the brother or sister to be similarly selfless.

Relationships are memorialized in our brains through words (thinking brain) and feelings (emotional brain). Have you ever met someone new and created an impression, or developed a thought, about how that person would behave or who you imagined that individual to be because you were reminded of a past relationship? This is your relationship history influencing current connections, and these activities of the brain often occur at an unconscious level. The memories and feelings that were stored in your brain come out to influence your current relationships and social interactions when triggered by a familiar face, behavior, feeling, or pattern of interaction.[4] If you are dating Ted and he does something that reminds you of John (from a past relationship), are you responding to the behavior of Ted or John? Intentional living requires you to focus and build self-understanding around your past relationships, which influence your current actions and social experiences.

Our thinking brains also define the meaning of a relationship and the intensity of connection that we attribute to specific individuals. What defines an acquaintance versus a friend versus a best friend? Our thinking brains not only describe for us the people in our world (*my tall, redheaded friend*) and the level of intensity of the relationship (*acquaintance to intimate partner*) but also hold for us a model—the elements and rules of what makes an acceptable relationship. Examples of relationship rules we may hold unknowingly in our minds include "People that lie do not make good friends," "It is not a good idea to date a coworker," and "Children should be seen and not heard." Next is an example regarding relationship intensity. You may tell your coworker about a fight with your spouse, but would you tell the grocery store clerk?

This example speaks to the level of familiarity you wish to give another person. Hence relationships of greater intensity often carry stronger influence in our lives.

At this point, I am not attempting to define what makes a good relationship but to outline how your individual thinking brain is involved in defining what you, individually, consider acceptable or unacceptable levels of knowledge or comfort with an acquaintance, friend, or family member. How do you define the rules and roles of the multiple relationships in your world?

Personal Development Activity

Defining Relationships			
Activity: Read each question below and, based on your level of comfort with the relationships defined in the columns to the right, mark a yes or a no for each level of relationship.	Acquaintance	Friend	Family Member
Ex: *I would feel comfortable telling this person about a problem I had a work.*	Yes/**_No_**	**_Yes_**/No	**_Yes_**/No
I expect this person to return my phone call or text message within the hour.	Yes/No	Yes/No	Yes/No
I would expect this person to visit me in the hospital.	Yes/No	Yes/No	Yes/No
This person would drive out of town to pick me up if I ran out of gas.	Yes/No	Yes/No	Yes/No
I would call this person to discuss an emotional problem, and this person would stop and listen.	Yes/No	Yes/No	Yes/No
This person would allow me to borrow their car.	Yes/No	Yes/No	Yes/No
I expect this person to share my religious beliefs.	Yes/No	Yes/No	Yes/No
I would gladly hold back this person's hair if this person threw up.	Yes/No	Yes/No	Yes/No
I would write this person a personal reference for employment.	Yes/No	Yes/No	Yes/No
Create your own question:			

The point of this exercise is not to determine right or wrong. There are no set of correct answers to the above questions. In fact, you may have another set of questions that define the various levels of relationships in your life much better than these few. The goal of this activity is to make you aware that your personal history, your experience of certain individuals, and your thinking brain all interact to influence your decision about how far you choose to let others into your interpersonal world. Who you feel comfortable with in a relationship is, in some ways, defined by how you label that specific relationship in your brain.

Emotional Understanding and Your Thinking Brain

In this chapter, we have been examining the activities of the thinking brain. Throughout this text, I will ask you to consider thinking and emotional experiences as separate events. However, in the real world, experiences of thinking are influenced by emotions and emotions involve thinking. More specifically, your emotional brain experiences a feeling and your body responds physiologically.[5] Next your brain creates a word or explanation for your emotional experience. The physiological experience of an emotion—the unconscious arousal or shutting down of the body in a response to stress—I will define as an emotional brain event.

So how then is the thinking brain involved in emotional understanding? Let's consider a real-world example. You are driving in a large city in dense traffic, and a car swerves in front of you and cuts you off. Your heart rate increases; your stress response is engaged; and you may feel panic, fear, or anger. Now, how do you label this event? Do you curse the other driver? Do you make a global inference about the ethnicity of the driver and blame a race of people for this action? Do you take a deep breath and express gratitude that an accident did not result?

For another example, imagine you are driving on a desolate country road. It is night, and yours is the only car on the road. Out of nowhere, a deer shoots across the road. You slam on the brakes so as not to harm the deer. You come to an abrupt stop, and the deer trots on as if nothing happened. Again, your stress response has been engaged; your heart races; and you may feel panic, fear, or relief. As you label this event, do you curse the deer for poor judgment?

Do you scream insults at the deer community for their smaller brains and for hogging the road? Or do you take a deep breath and respond with gratitude that neither you nor the deer was injured? How you define, attribute meaning, and create understanding of an emotional experience I will label as a thinking task.

To embrace intentional living, you must look at how you define emotional experiences along with the influences of such labels on productive living. Ask yourself questions such as, "When my stress response is in effect, is it helpful to use labels of hate?" It is true that the physiological nature of feelings happens to us, but how we interpret or define emotions is a choice. If the actions of another person are disturbing me and I become emotionally activated, do I choose to move toward and engage with that person, or do I walk away and seek something or someone more pleasing to me? This choice can only be made when you understand the individualized influences of relationship history, family culture, past emotional labeling, and your stress-response style. Thus there is much self-understanding required for intentional living.

Culture and Individual Difference

Culture is highly associated with how we understand ourselves. Culture can also be defined as the social rules that guide our behavior and interpersonal understanding. Culture encompasses family values, ethnic identity, gender identity, and connection to a nationality, among other factors.[6] Culture is individualized, determined from within (family values and self-understanding) and from without (community norms or national identity). One is never separated from personal culture.

Without a doubt, culture influences our thinking. Ethnicity, family upbringing, and professional identity are elements of cultural understanding that influence our thinking, or the labeling of events in our lives. Take for example a family system in which the emotional act of crying is labeled as a weakness and shameful. This is a family-based or culturally defined understanding of the act of crying, thus influences culture from within. These events will shape an individual's personal emotional understanding. The ethnic identity of the El Salvadorian, French, Lebanese, Taiwanese, Puerto Rican, or Ugandan may come with character labels for how individuals of each group think or act. Do you consciously or unconsciously demonstrate character traits that may be assigned to a nation of origin or ethnic group?

Here is an example of cultural understanding as defined from without. Specific professions may require acceptance of work-related practices for behavior and thinking. There is a defined military culture, academic culture, and hospital culture, which individuals in those professional systems can articulate. By this, I simply mean that certain ways of thinking are necessary and expected in certain professional roles. Again, the focus on your personal cultural identity, as influenced by labels and acceptable behaviors, is discussed here only to further self-understanding. I am in no way indicating that any cultural practice or set of beliefs is better or more adaptive than another. How do you think about or define your professional culture, family culture, and ethnic identity?

To further explore personal culture, consider the power of gender labels. There are culturally defined expectations for the behavior of women and men. These expectations often go unnoticed until a person steps out of the assigned cultural role. What thoughts run through your mind when you see a man in a skirt or kilt? Now, it is always important to consider when examining culture issues that *my* cultural truth and *your* cultural truth may be very different, and neither is less valid.

Personal Development Activity

Cultural Understanding		
Personal Cultural Systems	**Do's**	**Don'ts**
Ex: *In my family*	*Practice a shared faith, listen with respect to each other's feelings, yell when we get upset*	*Shame children to comply, abandon the senior community, judge others based on their looks*
In my ethnic community		
In my professional culture		
In my faith or belief community		
In my gender role		

As we explore intentional living in this text, you will be asked to think about what you believe about relationships as well as what you believe about yourself in relationships. I will help you examine questions regarding how much of your relationship success or failure is driven by what you think about yourself; what you think about others; and what actions you take based on the ideas that live in your head. To live intentionally, you must get to know your thinking brain, understanding what you believe, value, and stand for. You will then need to actively and intentionally behave in line with your beliefs. While this may sound simple enough, it is not as easy as thinking a thought and then letting it happen. Your thinking brain is also highly influenced by your emotions. In the next chapter, we will examine your emotional brain.

CHAPTER 4

The Emotional Brain

We have discussed your thinking brain and how it influences intentional living. In this chapter, we will discuss your emotional brain. Emotions are a complex aspect of the human condition. Our emotional worlds may not always be well understood—by ourselves or others. The goal of this chapter is to outline the tasks of your emotional brain and describe how it works, specifically as related to increased self-awareness and intentional living. Then we will look at how your emotional brain is shaped by your relationship history; how relationships influence emotional understanding; and the role of the emotional brain in your stress responses. We will also look at emotions within the context of the larger cultural expectations and your personal beliefs.

The Emotional Brain

Your emotional brain not only warehouses emotional memories but also attributes feelings to events. Take the simple event of losing your footing while climbing the stairs and stumbling. Your brain experiences the physical sensation (almost falling, uncertainty, lack of control) and then attributes or assigns a feeling. For example, your brain may attribute surprise: "Oops! I lost my footing and almost fell." It may attribute frustration instead: "Stupid carpet on the steps—how does anyone expect you to walk up stairs with carpet!"

Another attribution may be embarrassment: "Well, I am sure that I looked silly. I hope no one saw me."

It is not my aim to confuse the reader with semantics. Yes, the labeling of a feeling to an event involves the activity of thinking; however, for the purpose of building self-awareness, we will hold that the task of naming a feeling state occurs in the emotional brain. For the purpose of this text, the experience is as follows: you feel it, you name it, and you store it. These three events—experiencing, labeling, and remembering—will be attributed to the emotional brain.

Different individuals may attribute different feeling states to the same event. Back to the stumbling example, the various attributions can include clumsy, careless, silly, funny, anxious, ashamed, and sad. In addition, you may have a mixture of emotional responses to a single event. For instance, you may think, "I feel pretty foolish that I stumbled, but it was funny."

How does your brain know what to feel in each specific circumstance? Well, a great deal of your emotional understanding occurs in the early years of development.[1] Infants, toddlers, and preschoolers learn the language of feelings much as they learn the semantics or grammar (the tools of language) of their native tongue. Emotional understanding, like language development, occurs through experience, necessity, and repeated exposure. Let's consider the example of a three-year-old child who spills his milk. The parent becomes angry and shouts, "You should be more careful! What is wrong with you?" The child learns fear, shame, and self-defeat (*I am inadequate*). In the same situation, a parent who accepts that it's normal for a young child to spill his milk may calmly respond, "Oopsie daisy—everyone spills now and then. Get a towel and help me clean it up." This child learns acceptance, correction, and sensitivity of response from a caregiver. Thus when we are young, our experience with parents, teachers, peers, and the world gives us the language for feelings, which we later pair with our experiences.

There is still more at work. We learn by necessity—by the basic need to survive within our family system and the larger social culture. By necessity (the need to belong to a family system), children learn that various feeling states (regardless of verbal label) are appropriate or inappropriate in their environments. For example, some parents may accept the behavior of one child hitting a sibling in anger. However, the school will not accept that same child hitting a peer who took the child's pencil. At a more complex level, parents instinctively attend to their children's needs in order to move development forward and promote sufficient self-care skills. Infants do not feed or bathe themselves and therefore require parents' support until they master such skills. In the same way, infants do not comprehend the depth of emotional content until emotions are defined and labeled by parents or significant others in their lives.

Infants and toddlers are also learning appropriate emotional responses from parents and family members. These skills are learned through observation and repetition. Young children (birth to three years old) understand in an intuitive or unspoken manner what emotional expressions are acceptable and unacceptable in their families' culture. They repeat and hold on to the emotional patterns their families use frequently, and they let go of the emotional expressions that are not a part of their everyday worlds. Children are born able to speak every language in the world, but if specific sounds are not repeated and taught, the ability to create those sounds becomes more difficult over time.[2] In the same way, if emotions are not encouraged, repeated, or used in practical and realistic context during the early years, teaching of emotional content becomes more challenging with time. Of course, all is not set in stone in these early years; later life experiences also shape our emotional understanding.

This takes us to the concept of repeated exposure. Just as a muscle memory is formed through sports training and repeated practice, an emotional footprint is established in the brain over time by repetition of experiences. Erasing or changing these footprints will take repeated exposure, practice, and new experiences; you will need to alter perception, create new learning, and build new footprints in the brain.

One example of this involves the experience of a life-threatening trauma. If you have ever been in a natural disaster—such as a flood, hurricane, earthquake, or tornado—you may experience sleep disturbance, flashbacks, or an overactive startle response immediately after the dangerous event. These are normal reactions to an abnormal, and perhaps life-threatening, experience. For most of the population, such stress symptoms abate within a few months.

Your emotional brain was shocked by a high-arousal event, and recovery from that event takes time and repeated exposure to nonthreatening events. In other words, your brain needs repeated experiences of not being frightened, unsafe, unduly aroused, or overly stressed. After repeated experiences of calm and safe emotions, the fear reaction goes away. Until such time as another natural disaster occurs.

Your emotional brain is charged with the tasks of labeling an arousing or emotional event, creating a meaningfully organized record of that event in your brain, and then storing that event for later use. Turning to a computer-based analogy, your emotional experiences create a word document in the memory centers of your brain. Certain events will bring up that file and put it into play.

To expand the natural disaster example, imagine you were in an earthquake, and you have a file for emotions that go with an earthquake. You find yourself facing a flood, and your brain pulls out the file for earthquake. Your brain may use some of the content of that file or create new files to add to your emotional memory center. This is the act of creating personal memory for your emotional events. Remember that each person holds a personal emotional label or memory for their life events, and your emotional understanding may or may not be shared with others. The emotional memory of a snow blizzard for some may be joyful, as they recall a day out of school to play in the snow. The emotional memory of a blizzard for someone else may be fearful, as they were once snowed in for four days with limited resources.

Our emotional understanding is influenced by our experiences, family, friends, personal beliefs, and larger culture. Emotional understanding is a necessary survival skill. In order to survive within the context of a family culture or a larger community culture, a child unconsciously learns and expresses the shared family norms around feelings.[3] Repeated exposure to shared emotional understanding creates a footprint in your brain. You call on this footprint when similar people or events generate that emotion. Remember the child who spilled his milk? If he is always yelled at, what emotional understanding will be called up for him when his child spills milk? However, everyone does not share your emotional history and emotional footprint. Relationships become challenging when we assume that others share our felt experiences rather than honoring and seeking to understand others' unique interpretation of their emotional worlds. Add to this the understanding that your interpersonal experience with others will also shape their emotional understanding. This concept is explained in greater detail when we consider the influence of relationship history on emotional understanding. Relationship history influences your present behavior and felt emotional experience.

Relationships Build The Emotional Brain and Define Emotional Understanding

It is paramount that you fully understand how relationships are key in the definition and creation of emotional understanding. Parents teach their children social knowledge and emotional complexity as necessary for interpersonal success. We are driven to communicate and seek understanding from others. However, verbal communication is only a small part of the task. Our brains understand the nonverbal messages of vocal tone, facial expressions, gestures, and the rhythm or flow of communication before they gain command of the spoken word.[4] Additionally, before we comprehend the verbal meaning of another's communication, we have unknowingly interpreted a *vibe*, or felt understanding, of that person's nonverbal content. Infants as young as three months old can anticipate their caregivers' nonverbal cues and respond to the desires of parents seconds before a social cue.[5] Have you ever observed a couple communicating in a restaurant or on a plane? While you may not be able to hear the content, you can understand the nonverbal implications. You can tell if they are in a disagreement, if the conversation is tense or jovial. Often your observations will tell you if they are romantically involved or just acquaintances. Think of someone very close to you, someone you live with and experience every day (a child or spouse, for example). Can you surmise the emotional condition of your child, who has just returned from school, before a word is spoken? Can you predict the mood of your spouse upon waking, before any verb communication has occurred? How does your brain do this? This is your emotional brain unconsciously reading the nonverbal emotional cues of the other. So where does your emotional brain first learn about the emotions of self and others?

When you look in the mirror, you see yourself, which builds self-understanding. When you look into the eyes of an influential person in your life (a parent, best friend, sibling, or lover) you see the nonverbal social interpretation or meaning that the other person attributes to your behavior (relational ways of being with others). How others see you also influences *how you see yourself*.[6] Your emotional brain unknowingly encodes the impressions that others reflect back to you; next, the impressions of others are merged with your independent experiences to define the total complexity of you.

Emotions and relationships are forever intertwined. We learn the meaning of emotions through relationships. Parents and family members define for the small child the meaning of emotions as well as the family's culturally approved expression of emotions. As we mature, relationships with parents, siblings, peers, and partners (boyfriends or girlfriends) become the catalyst for the expression of intense emotional experiences.

Your emotional brain is where you hold the meaning of relationships (you see your child injured, and the pain you feel is experienced in your emotional brain). The sensations of infatuation, excitement, jealousy, betrayal, rejection, and delight are all found in your emotional brain. Your emotional brain holds the sensations associated with feelings. Remember, emotions start as sensations in the physical body. Relationship-based understanding (influenced by questions such as, "What is my role in this relationship?" and "What do I cherish about another person?") is worked out in the emotional brain. Sometimes the understanding of the sensation is effortless, and sometimes this understanding comes only through a relationship.

For example, consider that you are involved in a committed relationship that is moving toward engagement. You and your fiancé decide to announce your engagement at the winter holidays. Your older sibling informs the family that she and her partner will be having a holiday wedding this December. Now enters a complexity of emotions. You find yourself excited for your sibling, jealous that she has announced her plans before you could surprise the family, and a little angry as well. It is at such times—when our emotions are not clear even to ourselves—that we turn to others to provide a mirror of our experiences, to offer greater understanding of that which is felt yet not cognitively understood. It is within the context of a relationship that we come to know our emotional experiences. Our emotional experiences become richer when we share them with others.

Relationships build our emotional understanding. At the same time, the task of being in relationship (the ongoing back-and-forth verbal and nonverbal communication) helps to define our internal understanding of our emotions. For example, a toddler has trouble opening a small box. In this example, the parent labels the child's emotional experience. "You are getting frustrated. You keep trying and trying, but you still cannot open that box." This activity defines for the child his experience. As the child moves through development, he begins to self-define his feeling states. "I am so frustrated with this homework. It just does not make any sense to me, and it is due tomorrow." Here, the child is self-defining his felt experience. So we have defined two important operations. First the adults in a young child's life assist to create the meaning or definition of feelings. As children mature, they practice the emotional labels first given by adults and then redefine these labels through daily life experiences.

During adolescence, the brain goes through a dramatic developmental change, resulting in greater complexity of emotions and advanced cognitive understanding.[7] As a product of this developmental shift, many teens seek to shed the emotional meaning attributed by family and seek to redefine their self-understanding. You may ask, "How do teens relearn the meaning of emotions?" This occurs through relationships with peers and intimate partners. The teen strives to set herself apart from her past (family-defined emotional meaning) and develop a new self-determined personal understanding. At this point in development, peers become significant agents of influence as new personal meaning is taking shape. Just as the infant develops emotional meaning from the feedback of the parent, the teen builds an emotional library through interpersonal experiences with same-age friends, testing the role of intimate relationships and re-creating self-determined meaning for her emotional experience. An element of maturity is self-understanding as defined not just by your family history but also by your larger social network and your personal emotional experience. The self-attributions to events you create and hold in your mind—coupled with family, peer, and partner relationships—build this self-knowledge.

For example, take the adolescent who is raised in a community of strong faith. It is not uncommon for teens to explore various world religions and test out ideas of faith that differ from those of their family of origin. As a result of exploring new values and creating a self-defined meaning for faith, some teens may embrace a new faith. At the same time, other teens may return to their families' faith practices following a period of exploration. Thirdly, some teens may redefine their commitment to the family's faith tradition but practice in a different manner, denomination, or style. These variations all express the developmental activity of self-defining one's personal values and beliefs.

Your self-understanding is not a fixed point but a work in progress. How you see yourself along with what you value in life changes over your lifespan. As you mature, the influence of others wanes as you build your personal beliefs and goals as influenced by your personal life events and individual experiences. The following personal development activity has been designed to assist you in building an understanding of the influences of family, peers, and, finally, yourself on emotional understanding.

Personal Development Activity

Values Across the Life Span					
Timeline	Elementary School: 10 years old (Example)	High School: 17 years old	Young Adult: 25 years old	Middle Adulthood: 30s to 40s	Older Adult: 55 and up
What were/are your personal goals at this moment in time?	*Playing with friends and doing well in school*				
Which people brought you the most joy?	*Family and friends: Sarah, Janet, and Karen*				
What emotional events were too overwhelming to manage without the support of another person?	*Fear of scary events and the rejection of peers*				
At this point in time, did you put greater value in the views of others or in your self-understanding?	*I put more value in the views of my parents*				

What we have come to explain is that emotional meaning is created within the ongoing experiences we have with influential people in our lives. Our relationships stir up emotional *content*, and our relationship *context* helps defines for us the meaning of an emotional event. Our interpersonal experiences with others act to seal the fate of our emotional understanding. Let's consider emotional content and relationship context a little deeper with an example. In your relationship with a sibling, you may perceive that the older sibling gets more privileges or the younger sibling is spoiled. The emotional content may be jealousy, frustration, or anger. How does the relationship context play a role? Does the older sibling flaunt and tease the younger siblings about their privileges, or does the older sibling frame these additional opportunities as a rite of passage or a function of maturity that each sibling will achieve? The different relationship-based interpretations of the same behavior can alter the emotional understanding to the event.

When you have a successful event (a good grade for a student; for the adult, a new job, engagement, or home) you want to share the news with others, and their emotional excitement fuels yours. Friends who are not exuberant at our success are those with whom we stop sharing our positive life events. When bad things happen (car accident, family illness, job loss), we turn to caring individuals who will hear our pain and comfort us. In times of distress, we look for friends and family who can fully grasp our internal experiences and confirm their understanding by reflecting back to us a full comprehension of our distress. The act of others acknowledging our emotional experiences allows us to feel seen, heard, and validated in our emotional condition. These are the true friends, the honest listeners, the comrades in arms.

How does it feel when you share your distress (for example, a job loss) and the listener minimizes your experience with comments such as, "You can get another job" or "You didn't like that job anyway"? These comments, while offered to be helpful, do not mirror back your emotional condition and are therefore experienced as unhelpful. While in the depths of emotional distress, we may not be fully aware of our emotional condition or the personal options we have; the reflections of others offer clarity and self-knowing. This concept of needing others to validate our emotional experiences is explored in more detail in chapter 7.

The Emotional Brain and Your Stress Response

We have previously explained that stress happens to us. The origin of stress is as an adaptive mechanism designed to keep the species alive. Over time, and as a result of environmental and interpersonal influences, stress responses become associated with non-life-threatening events, such as fear of public speaking, social anxiety, or a phobia of strangers. These activities are unlikely to kill us, but our nervous system learns to respond from a place of overwhelming fear or anxiety, which ignites the stress response.

Think of a single event that might trigger your stress response (you are late for an appointment, you have misplaced a valuable piece of jewelry, or the air conditioning goes out in one hundred degree weather). First, understand that your stress-response system is housed in your emotional brain. Stress sends your emotional brain into full throttle, and you act solely on emotional understanding. What this means is that your thinking brain is now off-line (not working)—rational thought is rarely accessed in the height of a stress response. Under stress, the emotional brain acts unconsciously, impulsively, and without reasoning. Can you think of a personal trigger? How do you feel in your body when you get stressed?

The upcoming personal development activity is designed to help you assess where you may feel a stress response in your body. In the column on the left, you will find areas of the body. In the middle column are the physiological body reactions to stress you may experience—circle those that apply to you. In the column on the right, there is space for you to add personal responses not listed in the center column.

Personal Development Activity

Stress in Your Body		
I feel stress:	**I experience (circle all that apply):**	**Insert your own responses**
In my head	Headaches, tightness in my jaw, blurred vision	
In my chest	Rapid heart rate, tightness in my chest, shortness of breath	
In my stomach	Nausea, stomach aches, muscle cramps, diarrhea	
In my legs	Weakness, tingling sensations, heaviness	
In my hands	Sweaty palms, shaky hands or slight tremors	
In my feet	Feet tapping, feet sweaty, tingling in toes and feet	

The following is a very simple example of nonrational thought in a stress response. Have you ever said something you regretted when in a heated argument with someone you love? This is because stress unleashed the floodgates to your emotional brain, and all the safeguards that protect you from saying the wrong thing were disconnected. Once your emotional brain takes over, you cannot access social judgment, and anything is possible.

Hint: when you're agitated by your significant other and in a stress response, saying nothing may be your best option. A better time for an open discussion is when the thinking brain comes online for both parties.

A close family member—a parent, sibling, spouse, or child—can trigger your stress response with a single word, glance, or gesture. This is because your emotional brain is highly influenced by those you love; the emotional responses of strangers do not carry the same level of significance to our self-understanding. If a stranger does not like your new dress, you do not go into a stress response. If your spouse or sibling shares a negative opinion of how you look (because you have a new haircut, or were wearing a funny expression in a family picture), this feedback is more emotionally distressing. The emotional intensity of your relationship with a loved one leads to a stronger investment in their opinion of you.

Here are some considerations regarding stress and the emotional brain, as well as some additional key points. Stress sends your emotional brain into overload and shuts off the thinking brain. Stress is a primarily sensational, irrational, automatic response to a fear or anxiety trigger. Your emotional triggers are learned over time through experience or interpersonal shared understanding. For example, you may have a fear of bees from having been stung and experiencing severe pain; or you may have a fear of bees because your parent had a fear of bees, and every time you saw a bee, that parent communicated in words and actions the need to be afraid. Thus you learned to fear, or to become stressed out because someone else taught you this response style.

The point of contention is that a stress response is an automatic body reaction to a learned fear trigger. In your personal growth toward intentional living, you must begin to identify your fear triggers, which reside in your emotional brain. You cannot control your stress response, because it is an automatic physiological response. However, you can understand what sets off your stress response, be prepared for truly dangerous stressors, and work to tone down your reaction to non-life-threatening emotional triggers.

The Emotional Brain and Personal Culture

As individuals, we are all influenced by personal culture. Your personal culture is learned in your primary family system. Family systems reflect cultural, such as three-generation families, single-parent homes, same-gender couples. Much of cultural knowledge is communicated nonverbally or at an unconscious level.

For our discussion of the emotional brain, cultural understanding can be thought of as stored in your emotional brain centers. When asked to articulate our culture (we use our thinking brain to explain the nonlinear unconscious cultural knowledge), we often stumble over ideas that are limiting, such as "My family is Italian" or "We are Muslim." Culture is bigger than a single label and can be better defined as the unspoken rules that guide your interpersonal activities. We express our culture within our social interactions, both across and within cultural groupings.

Here is a social/cultural example: Am I permitted to hold my friend's hand, be that person of the same or different gender? In some family cultures, the answer would be yes and in others no. As cultural understanding is unconscious and individualized (your personal cultural norms are specific to you), when you encounter a cultural practice that does not fit into your cultural lens, your emotional brain might become triggered (your stress response kicks in; your thinking brain goes off-line). Sometimes the first response to a cultural practice that is unfamiliar is to call the practice bad, unethical, or immoral, when in truth, it is only unfamiliar—not within your cultural understanding. Lack of understanding can generate fear.

Let's break this down even further. The practice of having multiple wives is not common in Western culture, but some societies regularly practice this form of family style. Our emotional brains may kick in with comments such as "This is wrong," "It is immoral," or "It's against God." However, for children raised in such a family system, it is perfectly normal and a harmless practice of communal living. Consider the danger when a group of people, led by their fear of something different, make a global decision that one category of people are less than or without basic rights. What if we, as a group, were to demonize all left-handed people, or people with blue eyes or gray hair. It may sound silly, but in our history, we have attacked people with darker skin or those who practice a different faith, and our collective culture has allowed this to happen. This is the emotional brain out of control. Taking control of your emotional brain means taking personal responsibility for your unknown biases and fears of those that look, act, or speak differently.

How do you take responsibility for unconscious practices? You start by paying attention to your body and your brain. Learn to recognize your emotional triggers and start to acknowledge your biases. Accept that you have prejudices (outside-in labels of others) and then work to move beyond such limitations in your interpersonal experiences. Each person you meet is influenced by a set of cultural labels, which at times conflict with our inside-out expectations (personal culture). However, the self-determined inside-out cultural experience of each individual is deliciously unique and deserves honest expression. Taking charge of that which lives in the unknown recesses of your emotional brain is a primary task of intentional living.

CHAPTER 5

Your Emotional Brain on Overload

In this chapter, we will discuss the *emotional overload*, which refers to the moment in which your thinking brain is derailed by a flood of feelings, often intense distressing emotions. As a result of this deluge of feelings, access to rational thought is denied. The concept of the Amygdala Hijack was first described by Daniel Goleman in 1996.[1] Readers looking for deeper knowledge of Goleman's original concept may wish to study the text *Emotional Intelligence*.

We have discussed how your relationship history impacts not only self-understanding but also the emotions you experience intensely or in fleeting. Relationships define emotions for your thinking brain (the meaning you attribute to feelings), and these emotional memories, as tied to specific individuals, are held in your emotional brain. In other words, the subjective assumptions you make based on your experiences with your boss, your brother, and your sister in-law are held in your emotional brain and can lead your behavior. The meaning you develop around interactions you have with others also influences the way you behave toward them (your interpersonal world).

I experience my brother as a good listener, so I share information with him. I experience my sister as very judgmental, so I share less of my personal life with her. In addition, the way you *think* others feel about you also affects your interpersonal experience. If I think my partner is angry, I will just stay out of her way, as I hate to argue. In these examples, my behavior toward others is influenced not only by what they do but additionally by what I *think* they may *feel* toward me (my assumptions).

We unconsciously read the intent of others and, as a result, make judgments that influence our social interactions toward those people. This level of complex analysis happens at a preconscious level. In my interpersonal experience with another person, my interactions are impacted not only by the outward behaviors and words of the other person but also by how I alter my responses toward others based on what I hold in my mind (my assumptions) and what I believe others carry in their mind (their judgments) regarding me. Thus we are constantly influenced unknowingly by our assumptions of what others might think about us. Simply, we are "reading the minds" of others and acting accordingly. A great example of this is a first date or a job interview. On a first date, you are continually assessing the interest of the other person (what is he or she thinking about me) and making decisions (how forthcoming should I be regarding myself) based only on a brief interaction. A large value is placed on the assumptions you build about the personality of the other person involved.

Steps toward intentional living involve understanding one's relationship history. You have been asked to examine the personal questions: How do past relationships impact me today? How do I define using labels or ideas, the meaning of past relationships with family, friendships, or intimate partners? In other words, how are relationships memorialized in my thinking brain? What feelings are paired with past significant relationships in my life? What do I feel in my emotional brain when I remember a certain person?

The purpose of the next personal development activity is to aid you in identifying the emotional memories linked with significant historical or current relationships. In the far left column, you will find a relationship title. The center column asks you to describe the thoughts you associate with this person. In the final column, you are asked to list the feelings this relationship generates. The goal is to define the thoughts or thinking brain ideas about a relationship as well as the feelings associated with that relationship.

Personal Development Activity

How Do You Think and Feel About Relationships?		
Relationship	**What do I *think* about this relationship?**	**How do I now *feel* when remembering this relationship/person?**
Sibling: *Brother*	*My brother is five years younger than me. When I think of him, the words that come to mind are outgoing, friendly, immature, kind to others, not good with women, and in need of my support.*	*As I remember the relationship, I get a feeling of joy, caretaking, feeling helpful and loved as well as loving. I feel a sense of responsibility and a warmth or pleasantness.*
First intimate partner		
Sibling: _____		
Sibling: _____		
Best friend in high school		
Best friend at this time		
Father		
Mother		
Add a relationship here: _____		

Relationship history is held in both the thinking and the emotional brains. Furthermore, you cannot fully embrace intentional living without seeking to grow in self-understanding as related to your feelings. You have been introduced to emotional understanding as it relates to shaping the emotional brain. Individuals build emotional understanding by experiencing feelings in the context of a relationship that defines meaning for that emotional state.

A mother gives her graduating son a hug, tears streaming down her face. She explains that the tears represent pride in her son's achievement. This is an example of how the relationship gives context to the emotional expression and provides meaning. Emotional understanding is impacted by relationship history and simultaneously influences current social interactions. Now imagine the son in the above example as a father. His response to the graduation of his child is influenced by his past relationship history with his mother and the current emotional understanding developed in the present relationship. Let's move this example further: imagine the father has been very reserved in his emotional expressions with his son. If holding back emotions is the social norm for this father and son, the father may hug his child without the expression of tears. However, if this same father has created a more expressive emotional style with his daughter, he may shed joyful tears or offer a different exuberant expression in the presence of his daughter. This example shows that current emotional expressions are impacted by relationship history and emotional understanding, as held in the specific relationship, family, and community culture or environmental context to the event.

We have linked emotional understanding to expanding self-knowledge. Learning about your feelings involves deeply dissecting the foundation of your emotional state. You feel angry—why? Is it the event, the relationship, or the past meaning of similar events? Perhaps you are not angry but ashamed, and anger is how you have learned to express that emotion. Understanding your full emotional experience (using your thinking brain to build a fuller understanding of that which is felt unconsciously) is the work of emotional self-awareness. This task is an ongoing journey. Emotional awareness does not just happen without effort; it requires much purposeful and conscious engagement. The skills related to greater emotional self-understanding are explored in chapter 6.

Have you ever experienced a time when you felt overwhelmed by a distressing emotion—such as sadness, frustration, or jealousy—and the emotion seemed to come upon you without warning? Let's look at an example with Matt. Matt is calling the customer service department of a magazine company to cancel his subscription. After fifteen minutes of navigating the voice mail system, Matt is connected to a representative. Next Matt provides the necessary identifying information, such as customer number, and billing address. When Matt informs the agent he wishes to cancel his subscription, the agent states, "I must transfer you to the department that handles cancelations." Matt hears a click, a brief silence, and then a dial tone. He has been disconnected. Matt experiences the feeling of rage.

Let's use this to examine Matt's emotional awareness. Does Matt feel angry, frustrated, displaced, rejected, devalued, or disrespected? Some readers may respond that Matt has the right to be angry, but why and at whom. Did the agent do anything wrong? Did Matt do anything wrong? Who or what is he angry at—the phone, the voice mail system, the situation, the loss of time? Examining the cause of feelings of distress can help you in making intentional choices around how to respond to such situations. With a greater understanding of what has caused Matt's response of rage, frustration, or disrespect; he can intentionally move to get what he needs from the magazine company without letting his feelings get in the way of his goal.

To promote understanding of the emotions of an individual in the context of a relationship, I have explained the inner workings of the stress-response system. Each person's stress-response system is unique and influenced by both conscious and unconscious material. To build a deeper self-understanding of your stress response, you need to investigate your emotional stressors, or triggering events.

What are your emotional triggers? What or who helps you calm down or recover from stress? Children often need adult support to overcome stressful events. Their younger brains require the complex structure of adult emotional maturity to assist in building self-soothing skills. The developing neurological structures of the child's brain are not sufficiently coordinated to organize an intense emotional event and successfully self-calm.[2] Adults, over time, develop healthy and unhealthy methods of stress management. Stress reducers can include exercise, meditation, music, supportive friends, smoking, overeating, drinking, or violence. How do you manage stress? Intentional living promotes your development of healthy stress reduction techniques to enhance your self-understanding in the context of social interactions, or your interpersonal world.

The Moment of Overload

When initiated to full capacity, your emotional brain can interrupt access to your thinking brain, resulting in an emotional overload of rational thought. One experience that is universally distressing is betrayal. Imagine your intimate partner has an affair, or a member of your family borrows your car without permission and totals the car. These events violate your trust in the other, and the emotional impact of betrayal is highly challenging in the realm of emotional self-management. The emotional "stab in the back" sends your stress-response system from zero to one hundred in seconds. This is the moment of emotional overload. The experience of the individual in this moment might include seeing red, feeling flushed, being unable to access words to describe the experience, and experiencing thoughts of revenge or a desire to make others feel the same level of emotional pain the individual is experiencing. Has such an experience ever happened to you? Have such feelings flooded your brain and overtaken your thoughts?

At a neurochemical level, the emotional overload showers the brain with stress hormones. Think of the unpleasant side effects of steroid use. An emotional overload and the resulting surge of stress hormones can create a similar, though momentary, response. In summary, a strong emotional trigger sets off the emotional overload, stress hormones flood your brain like a tsunami, and you are overtaken by your emotional experience.[3] The rational, thoughtful, and planning part of your brain is now out of reach, and you are working solely from your emotional brain. The next personal development activity will help you define those personal, emotional triggers that engage an emotional overload.

Personal Development Activity

Emotional Triggers			
What events set off a stress response?	What are my emotional responses?	What are my thoughts?	How do I self-calm?
Ex: *Being cut off in traffic.*	*I get very angry at the other driver.*	*The other driver is a jerk.*	*Try to relax and be happy there was not an accident.*
Which people set off a stress response?	What are my emotional responses?	What are my thoughts?	How do I self-calm?

Examples of the Overload

Your emotional brain can be sent into overload by relationship history, emotional understanding, or violations of cultural norms. The next section will explain each in greater detail.

In the previous personal development exercise, you were asked to develop a list of personal triggers that set off a stress response. How do you know you are in an emotional overload? You will discover the moment of overload when you realize that you no longer have access to your thinking brain. Another way to think of the emotional overload is your stress response out of control.

The following is an example based on a relationship-history issue regarding Kurt and Chad, who are brothers. Kurt is the older brother, and he has always been more athletic than Chad. Kurt played high school baseball and earned an athletic scholarship to college. In Chad's eyes, Kurt was always more popular and successful, and his life seemed easier. Chad was the younger and slightly smaller brother. Chad was an A student who excelled in math and science. Chad received several academic awards in high school and gained a full academic scholarship to college. Chad completed his graduate work to earn a PhD in chemistry. Chad now teaches at the university level and Kurt has found success as a private business owner. Both men are in good financial standings and are able to support their loving families.

At a recent family party, Kurt arrived in a new car. Chad saw the new car and before Kurt and his family had entered the house, Chad was flushed with emotions of jealousy, inadequacy, and anger. Under his breath, Chad stated, "Kurt always has to be such a show-off." In Chad's mind, emotionally, he was the younger, awkward brother who did not excel in sports and was less socially active than his brother, Kurt. This emotional overload is the result of a relationship history in which Chad often felt inferior based on the successes of his older, more athletically talented brother. This relationship history influences Chad's current experience so much that it is hard for Chad to acknowledge his own achievements as a successful adult. Chad and Kurt's past relationship history influences their current emotional experience. Chad is allowing his emotional brain to lead his interpretation of his brother's current behavior. Can you think of a person in your life that might lead you to respond from a place more of emotion than thinking?

Emotional understanding can also trigger an emotional overload. This occurs when the unconscious meaning or label you have given to a feeling sends you into an intense emotional experience that halts your thinking brain. Once again, this is your stress-response system out of control. As an example, we will look at the experience of Jake.

Jake was the only son of Raymond and Doris. When Jake was eight years old, Doris died in a car accident. Jake's father, Raymond, had grown up in a tough urban community and managed to stay safe by limiting his emotional expression and stuffing his feelings away. At the time of Doris's death, Jake was very distraught emotionally and cried at the very thought of his mother. Raymond told Jake that to be a strong man, he could not cry and that crying was a sign of weakness. Raymond said to Jake, "To make it in this world Jake, you have to be tough and push those sad feelings away. No one likes a cry baby." This was the moment that Jake internalized the meaning of crying as a sign of weakness, for which his father had no tolerance.

Over time and with practice Jake learned to deny his feelings of sadness. Now, as a father and a husband, Jake enters into an emotional overload anytime his three-year-old son begins to cry. Jake's emotional brain takes over, and all he can say to his wife is, "Make him stop. I do not want him to grow up weak from being such a cry baby." In Jake's mind, crying is equated with weakness, and emotionally he cannot see the value of crying for his son. Therefore Jake's emotional understanding leads to an emotional overload when he sees his son or his wife begin to cry. This overload creates additional relationship problems for Jake and his family. At the very moment when his wife and child need his comforting and support, Jack cannot engage his thinking brain because of the resulting emotional overload. This leads to a significant rift in his emotional connection with his wife, who is denied emotional comfort at the moment of greatest need.

Does this example bring to mind any ideas regarding personal emotional understanding? For example, have you ever had a disagreement with a good friend or loved one whose outward expression did not honestly mirror your emotional experience? Comments such as "Well, why do you feel that way?" or "It is just silly to get so emotional about such a little thing" can signal a lack of common emotional understanding. What is significant about emotional understanding is that in some experiences, it is highly individual. We often want our personal emotions to be understood by our loved ones and friends, but others may not always share our inner emotional meanings; in a significant relationship, lack of shared emotional understanding can create communication problems.

Here are some helpful hints to the reader: seek to understand your personal emotional meaning of life events, and admit that it is individualized—and therefore not shared by everyone you know. For example, to some, teasing is jovial and to others it is hurtful. Try to be open to the emotional experiences of others and realize that everyone may not embrace the same emotional meanings that you hold dear. You may need to stop teasing the person who finds this behavior hurtful or learn to laugh with the good-humored jest of those who find teasing lighthearted fun. These differences in emotional meaning do not suggest that others are wrong, but you will need to take the time to build a shared respect for the deep emotional meanings that each person in the relationship holds.

Some violations of one's cultural norms can send the brain into an immediate emotional overload. Racial epithets are a prime example. Regardless of the derogatory term or group of individuals being vilified, these words send an individual into a raging emotional overload. This intense emotional response is fueled by the fact that such denigrating terms are often associated with a long history of abuse or social injustice. The feeling or emotional content of the term is greater than the word itself. Somehow, when a stranger utters a racial epithet, the emotional overload can lead to responses such as nausea and physical discomfort, the use of abusive verbal comments, or the desire to strike back in direct action against the violator. There is no rational—or thinking brain—reason that the views or opinions of a passerby should have such control over our mental abilities. As discussed in chapter 2, such violations of one's cultural values trigger feelings even before a thought can be formed; the resulting emotional overload emerges from the painful feelings associated with the thoughts, words, or actions of denigration.

Becoming Intentional

We have outlined how an emotional overload takes over your brain and sends the mind and body into a fully emotional (nonrational) response style. If an emotional overload is, by definition, out of our awareness, how then do we control it? Now that you understand what an emotional overload is, you can start to pay attention. First you must notice that you are in an emotional overload, which can be evident in your response style. By learning to pay attention to your brain and body responses, you can learn to identify an emotional overload. The emotional overload is a sensational experience, involved largely with your feelings, and often starts in the physical body. One way to tell you are in an overload is to pay attention to your felt emotional and sensory experience. What am I feeling in this moment—frustration, anger, shock, sadness, distress, an emotional void, or numbness? However, not everyone is fully aware of their physical body or sensory experience. Do you first notice how you *feel* in a stressful situation, or do you first identify what you are *doing*? Some readers may notice first that they are yelling (an action) or that they feel strong anger (a feeling), even though they cannot define the cause. Others will acknowledge the feelings related to a strong emotional experience before they fully interpret their behavior.

For someone who first registers feelings, an experience may look like this: I feel tearful and saddened; the news of my sister's car accident was overwhelming, and I do not know what to do. When actions come first, it might look something like this: I was screaming at my husband to stop driving so fast, fidgeting in the car, and squeezing my fist tightly when I realized I was terrified because I was unaware of my sister's condition as we raced to the hospital after her car accident.

It is important that you build the skills to identify when you are in an emotional overload. How do you feel? What are you doing? How are you treating others? How are others treating you? What is the indicator evident in your body, feelings, or behavior of others that tells you, your brain is now in an emotional overload? For example, you may see you are in an overload by how you feel, or because you experience yourself yelling (a specific behavior). You may first be signaled by the way others are responding to you. "Oh no. I made Terry cry with what was I saying or doing. Perhaps I am in an overload even now." Once you can identify that you are in an emotional overload, you next want to think back to the original trigger (what sent you into an overload?). Now, with that knowledge in place, consider the following:

○ These events or people can send me into an overload.
○ This is the feeling I experience when I enter into an overload.
○ This is what I do or how I behave in an overload.
○ When my spouse, child, or coworker looks at me like that, I know I am in an overload.

With the skill of figuring out what triggers your overloads, you still cannot stop the initial response, but you can work to derail the full experience of the overload and build the strategies to respond less intensely. Remember that your body and brain have evolved over time to function in this manner; deliberately working to alter your brain/body response to emotional stress will take time, practice, intentionality, and patience. Be patient with yourself and ask loved ones to be patient with you as you build new skills. Regardless of your actions or your feelings in a stress response, remember the power is in healing the relationship after a hurtful interaction. Your stress response may take you down the road of painful emotional overload, but how you seek to make right the wrong, repair the relationship, and build a spirit of understanding and forgiveness can keep relationships alive and healthy.

The upcoming development activity has been designed to assist you in defining antecedents to an emotional overload. You will be asked to dissect a life stressor and examine the individualized response styles in:

1. Body sensation (how do you feel)
2. Stress response (your response pattern to this event)
3. Actions taken (the behaviors you engage in during this type of overload situation)

While some general "moments of overload" are provided, space is also available for you to add personal emotional triggers to this list.

Personal Development Activity

The Moment of Overload Feelings vs. Actions				
Moment of Overload	How do I feel in my body?	What is my Stress response style? (Excited, Shut down, or Mixed pattern)	What did I do? (Actions)	Which came first—the action or the feeling?
Ex: *I could not locate my child in a department store.*	*Shortness of breath, heart racing, internal panic*	*Excited stress response*	*Walked quickly and vigilantly through the store*	*The feeling came first.*
Your girlfriend or boyfriend breaks up with you via text message.				
You lose your wallet on vacation.				
Your parent is seriously injured in a car accident.				
Write your own example				
Write your own example				

In the moment of overload, you are functioning on emotional energy, and your thinking brain will eventually come back online to question your behavior. Begin to consider the strategies you can engage in while your emotional response slows and your cognitive skills come back online. Some examples include deep breathing, walking or otherwise moving your body, listening to music, and thinking of something funny. The point is for you to find your own escape hatch out from the stress of an emotional overload. Self-calming activities are discussed in greater detail in chapter 7.

Once you can reconnect with your thinking brain, hold yourself accountable for your actions, assess any damage, make amends, and learn from your mistakes. Go back to the trigger and discover what sent you into an overload. Consider working to see the overload coming next time. Who or what helps you regroup and gain control (i.e., acts as your escape hatch)? If the overload can be seen as a dangerous flood zone, who or what can you count on to direct you to a safer, higher ground, and where can you find calm in the storm? Remember that caring and responsive people in our lives can often be our greatest resources in times of stress.

CHAPTER 6

Finding the Joy in New Heart Messages

The previous chapter introduced you to emotional overload. This involves the automatic and intense nature of the stress-response system which is held in the brain and felt in the body, occurring largely out of our awareness. Even in the throes of a stress response each of us can grow to learn more about our emotional response style and actively work to change or calm an automatic reaction to stress.

Affect management is a common psychological term used to define the strategies for taking control of your emotional responses. In this chapter, we will look at how to retrain your brain from a place of understanding the powerful influences of personal relationship history and the unconscious connections between actions and emotions. Keep in mind that thinking alone does not change feelings. Our feelings are undeniably linked to our relationship history, family culture, and learned emotional understanding. Simply learning to think differently does not undo a very complex and entrenched social/emotional history of development.

Altering your emotional experience begins with a deeper comprehension of the very foundations of your emotional understanding, from your first introduction to the meaning of feelings. Early emotional understanding is created in your family system, also referred to in this text as your personal family culture. What was the culture of emotional understanding (the meaning of feelings) and emotional expression (how and when to share your feeling states) within your family of origin? Young children begin this journey of emotional understanding (the linking of felt body sensations to verbal labels) from their parents and loved ones. Personal understanding of the experience and expression of feelings is tested in the teen years through interactions with friends and classmates. As adults, we find that past emotional meaning is helpful or less helpful as we grow in our new adult social world. We either begin to alter our emotional understanding and social strategies or we keep repeating the same social and emotional infractions with little understanding of what is not working well and why we keep creating the same relationship problems. As we continue to think about the concept of affect management and personal control of emotions, it's important to understand the concept of *heart messages*.

Heart Messages

Emotions are a necessary part of us. Feelings are embedded in the very blueprints of who we are as humans. How others see us and how we learn to see ourselves, including how we feel, shapes our self-understanding. This self-understanding includes our outward expressions of emotions and how our emotional states come to define us from within. The way our family and friends see us shapes how we learn to see and understand ourselves. We come to understand our emotions by the experiences we have with significant others in our lives. Heart messages become the lasting imprint of the ideas or values that others give us, which lead to our self-understanding.

Heart messages are those internal beliefs seeded by our loved ones. We hold onto these messages, which others use to define us, and define ourselves by them, even without conscious knowledge. Think of simple and seemingly harmless family taunts, such as "You got those big ears from your father," "You could fly with those ears," or "Here comes Dumbo—look out for those ears." Now weigh the previous messages against these next statements: "You have the eyes of an angel," "When you smile, your eyes smile with you," and "You got your caring and sensitive eyes from your grandmother."

The examples used here relate to physical traits; however, there may also be character attributes your family used to describe you. For example, "You are so stubborn" or "You're too sensitive."

The next step is to consider heart messages that left an imprint on your emotional understanding. As an example, if you grew up in a family in which self-pride was equated with conceit, you may have been encouraged to remain humble. An individual who holds the value of remaining humble may struggle with such job interview questions as "What are some of your strengths?" and "Why are you the best candidate for this position?" This is an example of an early heart message that is not helpful in the adult world.

Examples of other heart messages associated with personal attributes include "You are always so demanding, stubborn, and willful—I cannot stand to be around you," "Everything is such drama with you—it's the end of the world," and "You cry all the time and will never be tough enough to make it in this world." We refer to these statements, ideas, and ways of self-understanding as heart messages because they remain as lasting impressions on our hearts, shaping our social understanding and interpersonal behavior.

Heart messages are planted in the earliest days of relationship—from birth—and they continue to shape our self-understanding throughout life. Parents, siblings, family members, school mates, and intimate partners stamp these messages on our hearts. Sometimes these messages are empowering: "You are beautiful," "You are capable," "You are of value," or "I love you." Sometimes these messages are belittling or painful: "You are a disappointment," "I am ashamed of you," or "You will never measure up to my expectations."

Remember that our first language is nonverbal; early heart messages can be communicated not with words but with looks and gestures of acceptance or rejection. Think of when a grandmother gives her grandchild *the eye*, or when a father provides a disapproving throat-clearing sound to his child. These clearly understood nonverbal communication tools remain timeless. In addition, verbal and nonverbal messages can conflict. We have all experienced a situation is which someone's words tell us one story but the nonverbal communication is very different. There are glares that say, "I am disappointed in you." A shake of the head may communicate shame over a loved one. These nonverbal messages do not match spoken content such as "No everything is fine. I am not angry with you."

A negative heart message can grow in strength against us when our emotional resources are low, when we are stressed, or when we feel emotionally vulnerable. Let's think about the child with large ears. Many of us know and dislike the experience of being picked last for tag, baseball, or any activity. What happens to the child who is picked last and interprets this event as a result of the heart message "Those big ears are why no one wants you on the team"? Take it a step further: "I did not get into that college because of my big ears." "My wife left me because of my ears." Yes, this sounds very silly, but if you stop and think about the mishaps in your own life, you may find that you have attributed something negative to an early heart message. You may have held on to a negative message such as "You are lazy," "You are stupid," "You are ugly," or "You are embarrassingly shy." These traits may have been present at one time or perhaps never, but the emotional memory you hold of being defined as lazy or stupid resurfaces in the face of disappointment or rejection, such as when you lose a job or an intimate partner.

Emotions are not rational or evidence-based experiences. The meaning of feelings involves past experiences, labeling assigned by a family culture, personal experience of that emotion over time, and yes, the thoughts you assign to that feeling state. In a moment of emotional vulnerability, though, people often defer to what is easy and familiar. "Well, my family always said I was funny looking or not very bright, so that must be why I did not get the job." At such times of emotional distress, you may ignore or reject evidence such as peers telling you you're beautiful or being given an award or acknowledgement of your skills. We hang on to the negative, previously stamped heart messages and reject vast evidence to the contrary in times of emotional crises.

Heart messages stay with you throughout your life and tug at your soul, continuing to communicate those messages of inner strength or shame and disappointment. At the same time heart messages can be a source of inner strength and continued comfort when the messages are empowering and consoling. I therefore challenge you to be purposeful in your communication, verbal and nonverbal, to loved ones. Share a heart message of love, inner capacity, and abundant joy. "You are beautiful just as you are," "I love you always," and "You have hidden talents yet to be realized." Who left such heart messages in your soul, and do you pull on these loving comments even now in your life? The positive heart messages you deliberately seed in your child or your partner will last forever and provide strength in moments of challenge or times of sorrow. Today and every day, plant a heart message in someone you love. Furthermore, nothing is stopping you from offering positive heart messages to yourself.

A big part of undoing past negative heart messages is providing yourself with positive heart messages. If you are not the type of person to offer self-compliments, start by leaning on the positive comments others have given you. How do you currently take in, acknowledge, and hold on to the praise others give you? Some people minimize the flattering remarks of others with statements such as "Oh, it was nothing special." Or they may invalidate the comment by defining a master at the skill: "Yes, but I am not as good as Erika at tennis." Think of your own response to praise verses criticism. What do you most recall that significant others have said about you? Do you tend to believe and hold on to the negative comments of others, or do you celebrate the praise people give you? Why do you think this is? If you have trouble holding on to flattering comments, can you think about why that might be? Are you ready to, in an intentional way, celebrate your gifts and positive qualities as defined by the loved ones in your life? The following personal development activity is a step toward thinking about the heart messages you hold on to and how a heart message can build you up or tear you down.

Personal Development Activity

Praise vs. Criticism			
Person of Influence	**Statement of Praise**	**Statement of Criticism**	**Which idea do I hold on to?**
Ex: *Spouse*	*You are beautiful. You are loving and caring. You are a good provider*	*You cannot cook. That shirt looks terrible. I hate it when you nag.*	
Parents			
Best friend			
Boss			

You can start shifting your attention from negative to positive by simply focusing on any one of the above-listed positive comments. Intentionally make this positive statement your internal mantra for the day. Have you ever found a fortune cookie that stated just what you needed to hear and saved it for some time to remind you of something positive? This idea is similar. In an intentional and focused way, you should hold on to someone's positive comment about you. For example, "You are very creative" or "Nice job on the quarterly summary of sales." Carry this positive comment throughout your day. In the face of whatever negativity comes your way, just keep telling yourself you have competing evidence and trust in your positive statement for the day. Push negative heart messages out of your thoughts with opposing data.

This is just one idea for remaining committed to altering your personal view and solidifying positive heart messages. I encourage you to create a personal strategy that helps you hold new heart messages of competence and success.

Ingredients of the Heart Messages

As a review, heart messages are created through early childhood experiences, family culture, and emotional understanding. Science would argue that the self develops in infancy through the interactions and experiences of child and caregiver.[1] Early experiences of how caregivers see us lead to how we learn to see ourselves. Early experiences are saved in our brains as memories, both verbal and nonverbal. Heart messages are experiences of acceptance or rejection that are saved in our souls and later called up to provide self-understanding.

Family culture plays a role in heart messages. The unconscious transmission of culture is much like the subtle seeding of heart messages. We live the cultural agenda and values that are experienced within the context of our family setting. Similarly, we internalize the heart messages that loved ones speak over us in our youth. This unconscious internalization of heart messages mixed with the individual nature of cultural expression adds to the deep complexity of the human experience. Individuals are multifaceted expressions of various cultural influences, including ethnicity, region, gender, faith, levels of acculturation, and more. Heart messages can be tied to a cultural connection. Perhaps your mother was from the southern part of the United States and seeded the heart message "We southerners don't raise our voices in anger—that is a Yankee trait." If you grew up seeded with such a regional heart message, what is your experience of yelling—do you feel you have betrayed your mother, your southern roots, your culture? Do you feel you are now a bad person? How our family defines emotional behavior from a cultural point of view also influences heart messages.

We spent some time in chapter 4 discussing how people come to build a self-understanding of their emotions. Here it is important to add that our emotional understanding cements in many ways from early heart messages. When emotional responses—whatever they may be—are tied to shame, weakness, or a lack of self-control, it's easy to hold on to negative heart messages associated with those feelings.

Many of us have heard the statement that emotions are not good or bad. Emotions can be joyful or painful, but a painful emotion is not a bad emotion. However, when an emotional expression is labeled by your family culture as embarrassing or impolite, and this emotional meaning becomes stamped on your soul as a heart message, you now attribute a negative value to that feeling. Creating new heart messages can mean unlearning historical association of worth tied to a feeling. Remember that heart messages start in childhood, and it may take repeated practice, back steps, and restarts to make lasting change.

Finally, what gives heart messages lasting power is our reinforcement of past messages in current experiences. Let's go back to our child with the big ears. When he attributes his strikeout in Little League, the D+ he earned in geology, or his recent job loss to his big ears, he is acting on a past heart message. With repeated experiences and self-created, ongoing proof of past heart messages, the early association becomes a lasting tattoo.

Learning to Self-Calm

The steps toward greater affect management and training your brain to react differently to stressful life events involve increasing your self-knowing. First you must seek to learn about your stress response and identify your emotional triggers. Additionally, begin an internal study of your history of heart messages. What messages are effective, and what messages are stifling your relationship success? Work to erase or ignore unhelpful heart messages, and actively seek to plant new, more empowering heart messages. The above steps heavily involve your thinking brain, and lasting change must occur at both the thinking and feeling levels.

Furthermore, steps toward affect management involve working to feel better and actively practicing a different emotional state. Yes, the suggestion is for you to practice feeling good, restful, and emotionally calm. Begin by paying particular attention to times in your life that bring you joy. Not just over-the-top moments, such as the birth of a child or going on vacation. Attend to the everyday joyful moments: your child comes home from school and shares a fun interaction with a friend; your coworker comments on your new shoes; a car is pulling out of a space in a crowded mall parking lot just as you arrive; or, out of the blue, you receive an e-mail, Facebook post, or greeting card from a friend stating, "You make a difference in my life." In these times of joy, how do you feel? How does your body feel? What is your thinking brain saying? These questions build ongoing self-awareness. The manner in which your thinking brain memorializes a feeling state also leaves an imprint you can call up later to build self-understanding. I am suggesting that you begin to reinforce joyful or happy feeling in an intentional versus passive manner.

Furthermore, where in your life do you experience your joy? This will be different for everyone. Some readers may find joy with family, others at their work, some in leisure activities—playing or watching sports—and some in a faith community. You can find joy in multiple activities. Also, the same event can create more than one feeling; while you may find joy in watching sports, that same activity may lead to frustration or disappointment.

Most of us know what stress, fear, and anger feel like, but do we reflect on the joy in our lives? Do you understand how to create a feeling of calm in your life? To intentionally change how you feel, you must start by paying attention to the response your body provides to joyful feeling states. The next personal development activity asks you to think about the areas of your life in which you find joy and what joy feels like from within.

Personal Development Activity

Sitting in the Joy			
Provide an example of how you found joy in each context below.	How does my body feel?	What are my thoughts?	How do I retain that feeling?
Ex: *At work: I received a notice of appreciation from my boss.*	*Sense of warmth inside, shoulders relaxed, breath slow.*	*I am very good at my job and someone has noticed my skills.*	*Hold the feeling not just in my body but in my mind.*
With family			
With friend			
At home alone			
A leisure activity			
At work			
In faith			

Did you find this personal development activity easy or challenging? Are you a person who actively attends to moments of joy? Or are you the type of person for whom an event that is not stressful does not demand your emotional attention? Many people take for granted daily moments of joy and get easily overwhelmed in the emotions of frustration, anxiety, or depression. Knowing where and how you find your joy can help you in a moment of stress. This is the skill of learning to self-calm.

Here is an example to demonstrate the skills of self-calming. Beth is a forty-six-year-old, single female. Beth's mother died at the age of forty of breast cancer. Beth has been diligently receiving annual mammograms since the age of forty. After her most recent mammogram, the radiologist asked her to return, as there was an abnormality in the screening and the radiologist wanted to do a biopsy. This information sent Beth into a stress response, and she was immediately aware of the indicators of stress in her body. She started her self-calming activity by telling herself that the biopsy was a prevention measure and no one was saying she had cancer. Beth, who loves music and sings in her church choir, started to hum a familiar hymn that helped her to calm down. On the surgical table, during the biopsy, Beth intentionally decided to focus on only a positive outcome for the biopsy; she mentally repeated her hymn and remained calm during the procedure. Beth's experience offers an example of managing through a stressful event in an intentional way and actively making use of personal self-calming skills to overcome the sense of fear.

When you learn to be aware of how stress feels and how joy feels in your body, the next step is to rehearse feelings of joy and calm. Take small, daily stressors—you cannot find your car keys, or the light bulb goes out. Next, use these times to practice your calming skills, much as you would practice a fire drill. If you are not well practiced in the art of self-calming at the moment of a stress response or an emotional overload, you will not be prepared for action. Emotional calming can be learned. Intentional living requires a warehouse of techniques for combating stress.

The next chapter will focus on strategies for being more intentional with your feelings, thoughts, and behaviors.

CHAPTER 7

Fully Living with Intentionality

In chapter 6, we discussed taking action toward a healthier emotional under-standing along with a method for building positive heart messages. In this chapter, you will look at strategies for taking control of your interpersonal world. We will consider specific skills for self-calming and ways you can re-engage your thinking brain.

At this point, you should have a strong understanding of the influences of relationship history, emotional understanding, personal culture, and individual stress responses on daily living. The above life events (relationship history, emotional understanding, and so on) continue to live in the emotional brain and thinking brain while influencing our social interactions moment by moment. Now let's look at how we harness history to shape current behavior. You have learned about building self-understanding by distinguishing emotions as the product of current or past events, creating joy and finding calm in your day, and seeking to overcome a stress response in the making. We have discussed uncovering past heart messages and planting new positive heart messages. Now it's time to look at taking back self-control and not being a victim of your stress-response system.

Yes, stress happens to you; yes, your stress-recovery system is trained over time and largely out of your conscious awareness—but what can you control?

Often people focus on what they cannot do. Intentional living involves asking what you *can* do and taking full and dedicated claim to what is within your personal power to control.

One thing you can do is control your self-understanding; in other words, how you choose to memorialize an event or build self-understanding. Consider these two thoughts: "I did not get the job because I am not qualified" and "I did not get the job because I was overqualified." Can you see how the different attributions lead to different self-understanding? How you decide to build understanding and create meaning for events says a lot about you: Do you define problems and challenges as results of your failed personal attributes? Or do you define negative events as the product of poor circumstances? The latter approach makes the problem an external event, while the first approach turns the problem into a personality trait. You cannot change your personal traits, but you may be able to alter your external circumstances.

You can also change your experience by learning to identify when your mind and body are headed toward a stress response. In chapter 5, you were asked to identify emotional triggers, which could include traffic, certain behaviors from coworkers, or family demands that create stress. When you see an emotional trigger coming your way, what strategies can you use in response? You can change your environment, begin using self-calming techniques, or work to avoid the people who trigger you.

Let's consider this example: Carol dearly loves her husband, Frank. However, during football season, Carol can be assured that her husband will not be available to her or their family on Sundays. At such time, he will be dedicated to his football rituals at home or his local sports bar. At one time in the marriage, Carol would get upset, demand Frank make time for her on Sundays, and/or become disappointed when he failed to meet her expectations. As an *intentional* response, Carol can choose to accept that her husband will be unavailable on football Sundays. She can plan family events on Saturdays, make a weeknight date with her husband, or share Sunday brunch with a mother-daughter group. These options decrease Carol's stress because she has changed her expectations. Take ownership of what you can control, and choose to stop placing blame on the people or things that are out of your control.

You may find yourself in the midst of a stress response before you can actively avoid the triggers. In such a situation, what can you do? While you may not be able to easily take back control of your emotional brain, you can choose what you say. Sometimes when you're in a stress response, it is best to say nothing. It is highly likely that what you have to say is highly driven by emotion and perhaps not well thought out. How often have you said something in the heat of anger that you later wished you had not said? Statements such as "I hate you" and "I wish you were never born" are very hard to take back.

Actions can be more powerful than words, and fortunately, you may be able to also control what you do. Determine the safe actions you can take when in a stress response. Can you walk away from the situation? For some people, a quiet moment of listening to music or taking a hot bath is relaxing. Others may need to engage physically when upset. You can safely and actively work out stress by jogging or kick boxing. There are individuals for whom members of a faith community, family, or friends who listen without judgment can help in calming down. Begin now by creating a list of self-calming techniques that are personal and effective for you. Make a long list, as you will require a variety of techniques. You can reach out to these strategies when in distress.

While the above strategies are provided as suggestions, it is worth adding that intentional living and self-change occur in those moments when your emotional and thinking brains are both accessible. This means that the skill of selecting healthy attributions and creating an escape hatch for a stress response happen when you are not emotionally, financially, or physically overwhelmed. Your mind must be ready to integrate the needs of the emotional and thinking brains in order for the concepts of intentional living to become real in your daily life

Finding the Calm

Only you can determine what activities bring calm to your mind and body. In the previous chapter, you were asked to practice joy—to sit in the positive emotions of success and pleasure, building a sense of what positive emotion truly feels like in order to recreate these sensations when needed. In order to return to calm, you must know the feeling of calm. Each of you will have a personal definition, not just in words but in body responses, of what calm means to you. How does your calm feel, and where do you most find it? Some individuals practice yoga, meditation, mindfulness, or tai chi. These are all calming strategies, but they may not be your calming strategies.

The upcoming personal development activity has been designed to assist you in considering what helps you find calm and what might be a good practice strategy for building self-calming skills into your day. Recall the comparison to the fire drill earlier in this text. Similarly with calming techniques you must practice prior for the emergency situation.

First you need to consider the places you most feel calm and relaxed. These locations can be indoors or outdoors, and you are encouraged to consider multiple locations. Next list an activity, or activities, that helps you to relax. This is your relaxing activity, and it needs to have value only for you. Then add your feelings and thoughts when you are in this state.

Personal Development Activity

Sensory Chart for Calming Solutions			
Place: indoor, outdoor, away from home.	**Activity**: What helps me feel relaxed?	**How I feel**: How does my body feel and what is my emotional condition?	**What I think**: While in a state of calm or relaxation, what are my thoughts—the ideas that come to mind?
At the park	*Jogging*	*Body feels invigorated, emotions are whimsical.*	*My thought is, "Anything is possible."*
Coffee shop	*Reading*	*Body feels like a wet noodle, and emotions are at peace.*	*Thoughts are lost in the content of my novel.*

What did you learn about yourself from the above personal development activity? Hopefully you can find an activity or a set of activities that can be practiced regularly. I encourage you to schedule these self-calming activities into you day, week, or month. Just as you regularly brush your teeth or wash your car, plan to engage in emotional self-care according to a planned schedule. The goal of dedicated self-calming is to *intentionally* bring an emotional state of calm into your life. None of us will be able to avoid stress at all times. Too much of life is out of our control for us to live stress free, but we can work to find, practice, and recreate calm when needed. It is when you can find calm and downgrade your stress response that you can fully embrace intentional living.

Why Your Thoughts Go Their Own Way

Stress can sneak up on us when we have put a great deal of time and energy into things that haven't gone well. For example, you made a mistake at work; a past relationship brought up negative memories; or in a moment of anger, you said something very harsh to someone you love. You may tend to rehearse or relive whatever did not go as you had hoped. People play out alternative solutions and spend time considering "What if." Why does energy get caught up in what did not go well versus areas of success? Rehearsing and reliving a negative past does not change the event, and yet the brain puts a fair amount of energy in this task. Why?

First it is important to understand that the brain likes harmony or cohesion—when events and thoughts fit well together. Inconsistency in the brain (thoughts versus experiences) creates emotional tension, and in an effort to ease distress, we seek to integrate troubling events by replaying them with new solutions. As an example, when someone does not share your opinion, you might spend a great deal of energy attempting to convince that person that your view is correct. Because that view is correct for you, your brain is somewhat unbalanced by the idea that someone else cannot appreciate your position.

This is the circumstance with Ann, a recent high school graduate who wants to defer her admission to college and work overseas for a year to gain life skills. Ann's parents do not share her view. This creates emotional distress and disparity for Ann and her parents. Why is it that the other party just cannot see that *my* view is correct? Now in truth, each person's view is true for that person. What is most distressing is when others choose not to honor or acknowledge our views as having merit.

Redirecting brain energy is the key. When you cannot integrate or add to your experience a distressing emotion, idea, or opinion of another, you might find yourself replaying the events, or conversation over and over. You are reliving, rehearsing, and hoping to fit the idea into your world view thus matching your current emotional understanding. However, the more you wrestle with these differences the more energy and perhaps emotional distress you self-create, much like trying to force a piece from puzzle A into a slot in puzzle B. What would happen if you just stopped trying and put the puzzle aside? Can you let go of that which others do not understand or respect about you? Can you stop needing to make others see the world through your eyes? Can we learn to respect that a different opinion is not the wrong opinion? What a gift it would be to others if we could simply accept that their personal life experience, inside-out culture and world view has value to them, even when we do not agree. Consider this, can we find the gifts in those that annoy us? Furthermore, can we train our brain to restate the events that were successful in our day, rather than the ones that did not work as we planned? Consequently we do rehearse our relationship failures hoping to organize the event in our brain thus creating harmony. However, what would happen if we just accepted that some relationships will be out of tune with our needs and be OK with that? Stop reliving what did not work and start underscoring what was a success. How might your life be different if you ended each day thinking about what you did well versus what you wish had been different? Give it a try for just one week and see if your brain and your soul finds calm.

Creating Repair/ Moving Forward

None of us can change the past. We should embrace that our past relationships are an important part of shaping who we have become, however, we are not limited by our past and we can take the reins to direct our future. The time you take to read this book is a new moment. You have a long history behind you that has influenced your brain, social understanding, and interpersonal relationship style up to this point in time. That past will forever be a part of you. However, today you can intentionally act to not allow your past to guide your future. While there is no firm set of instructions that can magically change your life or alter the course of your future, I have prepared the following set of steps to assist you in thinking differently about past mistakes and future opportunities. Some may find these steps helpful, others may not. Use these ideas as a starting place as you create your own solutions. Today can be whatever you make of it.

Personal Development Activity

Today's Date:_____

This Moment in Time			
Person or Event	**History**	**Person or Event**	**Future**
Name significant events from your past that have influenced your present.		List events you are looking forward to that will define who you wish to be.	
Name past life events that were important in your past cultural understanding.		Name life events you will take into your future that are linked to your current cultural self-understanding.	
List the people who have influenced your past in a positive or negative way.		Name the people to whom you wish to remain connected in the future, as they empower you to build self-understanding.	
List past events that your brain rehearses and you find hard to let go.		List new life events you seek to create and positive memories you hope to make.	
List relationship traits of people from your past that you do not wish to experience again.		List relationship traits you want and need in new personal relationships of support.	

It is suggested that you put a date on this personal developmental activity so that you can complete the process again at a future date and track the changes in your perspective. What are the elements of your past that no longer support your current self-view or future goals, and are you ready to let them go? What aspects, people, or events will lead you to the future you desire?

Steps to creating personal change

1. Forgive yourself for past mistakes. Everyone has made mistakes in life; the task is to learn from those mistakes and make different choices. Mistakes teach us about ourselves and the type of people we want and need in our interpersonal lives.

2. Stop holding on (by rehearsing) to relationships that harmed you physically or emotionally. If someone misused your friendship or trust, the responsibility belong with that person. Your culpability ended when you ended the relationship. Do not keep alive someone who harmed you by reliving the past. If you made a mistake, learn from it and return to step one. Forgive yourself.

3. Find people who emotionally support you and socially enrich your life. Seek relationships that offer coherence to your brain. If a relationship or event brings conflict to your brain, perhaps this is a relationship or situation in which you may not want to invest. Do your current relationships bring you a greater measure of joy or distress? If the equation is not what you need, how do you work to change this?

Finding the Right Relationship

We all need supportive relationships—with understanding family members, friends, or life partners—to facilitate social learning and emotional understanding. Relationships show us who we are in the eye of others, and they provide a necessary appraisal of our successful interpersonal skills. Consider the child who is praised in school for her success in math. This provides the external validation that she can succeed. As a result, she begins to cultivate a self-image of a successful math student. In contrast, image the boy who is told he cannot draw. Despite an internal drive toward artistic endeavors, this child may shy away from such tasks because the external messages tell him not to try.

In support of optimal developmental outcomes and strong social emotional skills, children need to have their world view shared by another. The child's true experience must be seen, felt, and explained through the filter of a mature and emotionally organized adult. Keep in mind that maturity is more than being of a certain age. Moreover, the science of the brain tells us that the evolution of cognitive maturity results from the mixture of quality relationships children, teens, and young adults have with significant others (parents, teachers, adult role models, and even peers).[1]

In truth, it is the very nature of the human condition to share our experiences, our lives, our values, and our world views with like-minded others. We find friends who value what we value. We share activities with people who enjoy the same things we enjoy. Relationships involve validation of who we are and how we see ourselves. People don't enjoy being in situations in which their personal opinions or values are not appreciated, accepted, or respected.

Consider this, you may choose to be a vegetarian and have friends that are nonvegetarians. A friend who selects a restaurant with various meat and vegetarian options shows respect for your values. Now if your friend chose a steak house for dinner and made a comment such as "This is America and we eat meat—deal with it," would you choose to hang out with that person often? This may sound like a silly example, but often in interpersonal interactions, we deny the real-world experience of our children, friends, or partners. Messages such as "Don't feel that way" and "You should not think that" and "My belief is better than yours" are constant and at times well meaning.

For example, when you see a friend in pain, in an effort to make the friend feel better, you might offer minimizing statements. Similarly, after your friend breaks up with a fiancé, you might offer words such as "You will be OK" or "You are better off without that person." It is your desire as a friend to help the other person feel better, but in the process, you can end up reducing or rejecting your friend's true experience. In this moment of grief and loss, your dear friend needs to be seen, heard, and felt. In your words and nonverbal actions the message should communicate (*I see you in the manner you see yourself and can reflect that back to you; I hear what you need from me and try to offer it; I share in your feelings even when painful to help get you through the struggle*). The gift the listener brings is to see what the speaker sees not to comfort them out of their sad feelings.

It can be hard to sit with and share the pain of a loved one who is experiencing a negative emotional condition. At times, as a listener, your capacity to tolerate another's devastating life experience can become overwhelming—when sharing the pain of the loss of a child or a terminal diagnosis, for example. When we extend ourselves to fully be with others in their suffering, we share in the feelings and experience of their emotions. Our own limitations in hearing and holding the pain of another may drive us to indirectly encourage the speaker to stop sharing or go to someone else for comfort. Perhaps we conveniently make ourselves less available, and others come to expect limited emotional availability from us. So how do you fully and truly see others and respect their emotional conditions and inner experiences? The capacity to listen at this level in support of your loved ones requires emotional effort. This form of emotional listening does not always come naturally, but it can be a great gift to another in deep emotional pain.

Next, how do you communicate that you see someone's real experience? Not the experience you imagine or want to see but the true and honest experience? When others tell us, "Oh yes, Kelly is nuts if she thinks the Oakland Raiders are a better football team than the New Orleans Saints," then our internal reality or world view is acknowledged. From here we can feel accepted or fully seen. This very simple example shows how the speaker is looking not only for someone to share their opinion, but more importantly to say, "Yes, your experience of the world is legitimate" or "Your reality has merit." Below are some examples of seeing another's true experience:

- I see that this is very painful for you.—*I see your true emotional condition.*
- I can hear in your story that this is more than the loss of a relationship and that the deeper meaning of that relationship is also lost.—*I want to better understand what this event means for you both personally and emotionally.*
- I feel sad that you must go through this, but I am here for you.—*I cannot take the feelings away, but I can share the weight.*

This level of shared understanding is needed from birth to death. It is rare and hard to come by in everyday social interactions, mostly because it takes time, emotional energy, compassion, and honest expression. In our fast-paced, high-tech world, such ideals can be hard to accomplish. Loneliness results from not having others mirror back the very existence of your experience in the world. The old saying goes, "If a tree falls in the woods and no one is a present, does it make a noise?" Similarly, if our experience is not validated by another, what meaning will it hold for us? The interpersonal meaning of the experience is created in the sharing of the event with another. As individuals, we yearn to be a part of a group; to belong; to feel someone has joined us in the emotions, sensations, and thoughts we are going through. Your capacity to be socially relational and truly emotionally responsive to others is a gift from your very soul. Are you willing to make the time to give these gifts to your loved ones, to fully share your soul with another?

Giving this level of emotional support and personal understanding requires self-understanding, patience, and emotional energy. Therefore, it is a gift that is not given in casual relationships. This type of support is offered to your dearest loved ones, and it is not required twenty-four/seven. However, it is necessary when your loved one is having a moment of emotional overload or feeling particularly vulnerable to past negative heart messages. You can better give understanding when you receive it in your interpersonal world.

Do you currently have friendships or other social relationships that give you this kind of feedback, emotional support, and self-understanding? If not, why not? How do you create them? As human beings, we are designed to be social; we crave emotional understanding. You are more whole, personally successful, and fulfilled when you know you are seen, heard, and felt by another—more specifically, by another soul who genuinely cares about your success, emotional safety, and overall well-being. Intentional living is supported by good relationships with caring others who can see, hear, and fully feel your experience without judgment.

CHAPTER 8

Creating Relationships that Support Intentional Living

Now the questions are: Who do you want to be? How do you want others to experience you? Do you want to be driven by your past relationship history, reliving the same relationship experience, even if the only similarity between the current and past relationship is the internal meaning you give to this life event? Can you risk thinking differently and trying to create new or a different emotional understanding of events? Are your past emotional attributions of life events the only ideas of value? As the world changes, life moves forward, and your physical and personal development matures, can you envision new emotional meaning? Do you want to hide your personal culture or celebrate it? Do you have a strong connection to your personal cultural values (inside-out culture) and how do these values influence your interactions with others on a daily basis? Are your personal cultural beliefs evident in the way you treat others? Do you wish to express your culture in that way? Are you willing and ready to invest time and practice into the management of your stress responses?

The goal here is to learn how to manage the controllable responses of your brain, for there will always be brain responses you cannot control. Furthermore, stress can have damaging consequences, including poor health and early death.[1] A commitment to improving stress management might just extend your life.[2]

Personal Development Activity

Who do You Want to Be?		
	Your goal	**Your action plan**
What is your personal goal for relationships?		
As you increase your emotional understanding, how do you wish to be different in the way you express or share feelings?		
What aspects of your personal culture do you wish to make public?		
What aspects of your personal culture do you plan to keep private?		
How will you better manage your stress responses?		
Can you forgive yourself for past mistakes, as you learn from various life challenges?		

Once you have committed to who you want to be in your relationships with others, consider how you want others to experience you. Which relationships from your past left a positive impression on you? What do you most remember about the way those relationships made you feel—or the heart messages planted by those who unconditionally loved you? Do you want to leave that level of joy in the minds of those with whom you are closest today? If so, make an intentional step to be an individual of significance in the life of another person and leave a positive memory by sharing that others are of value in your world.

If you are not pleased with your current emotional understanding, change it. Clearly, that is easier said than done. However, why must you hold on to emotional definitions that were started by your parents thirty or more years ago? Yes, you can change your emotional condition, but it is hard work. It is purposeful, deliberate, focused, and involves the integration of the emotional and thinking brains. This means you must learn to feel and then stop to take the time to assess those feelings. Are your feelings driven by your relationship history, past emotional meaning, or your strongly held cultural beliefs—or are they products of the current relationship? Once you have considered the source of your feelings, you can consider an action. This personal reassessment takes self-understanding and patience. However, it can keep you from reacting from a place of historical emotional meaning. Changing your emotional understanding is a daily task. You will have moments of success as well as setbacks. But the final letting go of past emotional baggage is well worth the effort.

Personal culture is just that: It is your individual expression of the multiple cultures that influence you.³ Your inside-out cultural experience is influenced by various factors, such as ethnicity, gender, faith, and nation of origin. At the same time, you get to define how much of your personal culture you choose to draw from each of these focal points. For example, is your expressed culture more highly influenced by being Catholic or from New York? Being a hockey fan or a musician? Culture is about values and how we express these values in our daily interactions with others. What areas of your personal culture do you wish to make public, and which do you hold as private? How do you wish to share your culture with others? Who do you want to be? How do you want others to experience you?

In order to fully benefit from this text, you must be ready to actively shed past negative heart messages and willingly embrace a new way of being with yourself and others. Change in the self—your way of thinking and being— is a very complex process. Interpersonal change is an active, not a passive, activity. Consider how many years it took to become *who* you are and *how* you are in relationships. Self-improvement will not come to you; you must go out and intentionally seek to create a new social foundation. A change in your social world involves making shifts not only in how you think but also how you interpret or understand your emotional experience (internal emotional understanding). How you store emotional events (memorialize relationships), both the positive and negative components, influences your personal development. No book creates interpersonal change alone. You must work toward constructing the necessary change you want for your life. This change involves an examination of yourself as well as a realistic assessment of the people you wish to keep emotionally close to you.

If you are seriously hampered by interpersonal distress, debilitating depression, anxiety, or addiction—or if you are engaged in abusive interpersonal relationships—I recommend professional help from a skilled psychotherapist who has advanced training in interpersonal neurobiology. Concerning symptoms include severe emotional distress, such that you don't want to get out of bed; lack of appetite or a desire to overeat; a lack of positive emotions in relationships; and finding yourself too nervous to focus on the task of everyday living (work, school, household chores, or parenting tasks). In addition, repeatedly finding yourself in social relationships that are physically or emotionally abusive indicates the need for professional help. You may wish to call a local hotline for Behavioral Health Services, Partner Abuse or Suicide Preventions. It is never too late to seek help.

Each day you have the opportunity to make a choice for just that day. Will you live chained by your past and anxious about the future, or will you focus on the current moment in time, making the most of every present possibility? Your emotional brain lives in the past as guided by relationship history and past emotional understanding. Your emotional brain functions to store past emotional content and make use of it in current relationships. However, old emotional garments may no longer fit you well in your current lifestyle. Now, your thinking brain has the option of living in the past, the future, or the present. The gift of intentional living is choice: When you take the time to think things through and gain insight, you receive the gift of intentionally choosing your actions, your thought processes, and ultimately how you want to live your life.

What is your choice in the moment of an emotional overload? What is your choice when relationships are distressing, or emotionally unsatisfying? The ongoing work of intentional living is about personal choice and taking control. You can blame your past, your parents, or your old mistakes for only so long. You have the potential each day to create a new canvas for your life, making the vision brighter, more satisfying, and undeniably yours. Your past will impact your current feelings and behaviors, but your past does not determine your future. To live intentionally, you will need to actively seek each day to live not in your past but in your current life experience.

Throughout the book, I have offered exercises and suggested activities to help you think, behave, and experience your world differently. If done regularly, this will lead to new habits, new brain connections, and new emotional memories. You are never too old to change your emotional or thinking brain, but it will take dedication and time.[4]

Relationships Can Heal

Our bodies and brains crave interpersonal connection. By the very nature of the human condition, individuals seek human relationships. Relationships are the mechanism through which our social and interpersonal development unfolds.[5] Relationships nurture your self-esteem, and it is by the way others reflect back their experience of you that you come to better understand yourself—from infancy through adulthood.[6] It is often said that the eyes are the windows to the soul, but more importantly, the eyes of our loved ones provide a mirror for self-understanding. Relationships teach us how to be with others, show us who we are, and feed our very souls. You can learn to use positive relationships to help you on your journey toward self-growth.

Relationships are a powerful tool for personal growth, self-understanding, and emotional repair. Not only should you know how to seek relationships that can help you heal and offer you emotional support but you should offer a relationship that is healing and gives hope to others. It is a normal part of the human experience to desire to be truly seen and fully emotionally understood by another,[7] but more specifically by someone who demonstrates both caring and nurturing for us. This translates to being emotionally understood, by a parent, a dear friend, or an intimate partner. At our core we desire that our loved ones will know and reflect back to us our deepest inner needs for support, strength, and understanding. This level of understanding and healing can greatly assist you on your path to becoming more intentional.

There are some basic qualities that you should look for and offer in a healing relationship. First, successful relationships should not cause emotional harm. To this end, be a person who seeks to offer emotional safety to loved ones. Emotional safety involves accepting the emotional condition of the other person. When your child tells you "I am afraid," do not say "You have nothing to be afraid of." Stop and listen with your full heart, and honor your child's real experience of fear. Before you try to fix the fear (or the feelings of someone else) say something like, "That sounds important to you. How can I best help you?" This shows not only that you are able to listen to the feelings of another but also that you are willing to work with that person to create a solution rather than simply offering a quick fix that may or may not work. Emotional safety also involves supporting others through an emotional overload or assisting others in the management of their stress responses. As an example, if your child is afraid of Santa Claus, you would support emotional safety by avoiding Santa's Village at the mall during the holiday season. Emotional safety is evident when we do not actively push someone we love into a stress response. Who listens on that level to your emotional state and stops to hear you without judgment or a quick fix? Who can serve as an escape hatch, or higher ground in the storm of an emotional overload? If you do not currently have this level of relationship support, I recommend you work to find it. Ongoing ingredients of a healthy relationship include emotional safety and mutual respect.

Mutual respect is found in a relationship in which you are accepted by the other person just as you are. There are no conditions—hence the term unconditional love. If you need to change your personality—your genuine interpersonal way of being—or deny your personal beliefs to be in a relationship, is this a relationship worth participating in? Sometimes—such as when you're at work, in school, and even in a family—you do not get to select with whom you will be required to relate. In life you will be obligated to accept that some people may not respect your emotional experience and they are still going to be a part of your life. However, in the area of friends and intimate partners, you do get to select the qualities that matter for successful relationships. Respect is yours to give, and you are never compelled to accept disrespect. Yes, others can disrespect you, but you are not required to hold on to a negative heart message seeded by a coworker or ex-partner. While another's disrespect or negativity is free to give, you are equally free not to make it a part of your emotional memory. Reject that budding negative heart message.

In addition to emotional safety and mutual respect, reflection is needed in relationships of healing. Reflection is the task of being seen in your true life experiences. We come to know ourselves by the manner in which others mirror or reflect back their perceived experience of us. When significant others see us as capable, we internalize a sense of competence. When loved ones tell us we are inadequate, we develop a self-image of inner lacking and imperfection. This becomes a heart message. The genuine emotional reflections of others enhance our emotional self-understanding as well as provide a model for relating to others. Relationships that heal will offer you emotional safety, mutual respect, and the reflection or validation of your experience.

When your experiences, opinions, and feelings are authenticated—reflected—by another, you most likely feel grounded at your inner core. At the same time, when your reality is misinterpreted, called into question, denied, or refuted, you will often feel invalidated. Let me be clear, I am not saying that a person may never disagree with someone else; I am saying that each person's individual experience is real and true for that person. However, there are disagreements in life. When considering one's experience, we must distinguish facts from opinions and feelings. An internal experience is based on a subjective (non-fact-based experience), and yes, that is the individual's truth. However, a fact is a measurable and objective truth. The color red is qualitatively different from the color blue, and that is a fact. If one prefers the color red to the color blue, that is the individual's subjective opinion, and it would be correct and true for that individual. At the same time, if someone happens to be color-blind, then red and blue may look the same for that person, and this becomes the true lived experience of that individual. So where does intentional living fit in? This becomes important when our inner truths conflict with those of others, such as family members, friends, or intimate partners.

Relationship conflicts often occur when one partner feels that the other does not fully see or validate his or her inner truth. When your spouse says, "I am so sad about missing that movie" and receives the response, "Well, there is no reason to be sad—we will see it next week," your spouse's experience has not been honored. A more validating response would be "I can see you are very upset about the movie" or even sharing your feelings while acknowledging the other's needs: "I am not sad, because I am looking forward to going with you next week, but I can see you are upset by this." When the teen says to his parent, "But I have to be at the hockey game or my friends will think I am a loser," this is the true experience for this teen. Your teen is angry and upset. He wants his parents to acknowledge the legitimacy of his felt experience. You can validate his feelings of anger and frustration, without agreeing to his demands. Hence, validation does not equate to agreement.

Finally, healing relationships are collaborative in nature. This means that both parties get their needs met in the relationship, though perhaps not at the same time. The point is that in a healing and nurturing relationship, your needs are attended to by a caring other while you lovingly care for the needs of that person.

As a note: this level of equality is not present in a parent-child relationship, as the relationship is inherently inequitable. Nevertheless, with equally emotionally available adults in a friendship or intimate partnership, collaboration in the realm of supporting each other leads to healthy social relations.

Living Intentionally

As together we have explored the concept of intentional living, you have been asked to do a decent amount of introspection. Change begins from within, and only you can be responsible for your personal change. Toward creating that change, it is important to understand how both your thinking and emotional brains work together, and sometimes separately, to influence your social world. These are powerful factors that impact the history and ongoing development of the thinking and emotional brains. These factors have been presented here but will need to be further explored at an individual level. The factors of relationship history, emotional understanding, stress response, and personal culture are significant to daily life and deeper self-understanding. Are you willing and able to take charge of your inner world as it impacts your outer experience? Remember people can be your greatest advantage or your downfall. So choose your guides on this journey of self-discovery wisely. The journey continues, and the roller coaster of life will take many turns. Navigating the course is up to you. I only hope that the practice of intentional living provides you a compass for a smoother, steadier ride.

ENDNOTES

Chapter 1
None

Chapter 2
1   Phillips et al. (2003); Hamann (2001).
2   Perry et al. (1995).
3   Lilla & Turnbull (2009).
4   Anderson et al. (2006); Burke et al. (1992): Cahill et al. (2003).
5   Addis et al. (2007); Buckner et al. (2008).
6   Gross (1998); LeDoux (2000).
7   Siegel (2012); LeDoux (2003).
8   De Kloet et al. (2005); McEwen & Gianaros (2010).
9   Spencer-Oatey (2008); Matsumoto & Juang (2012).

Chapter 3
1   Carter (2014).
2   Fuster (2008).
3   Mitchell et al. (2005); Adolphs (2001).
4   Schacter et al. (2007); Bar (2007).
5   Andreassi (2000); Bradley & Lang (2000).
6   Valsiner (2007); Matsumoto & Juang (2012).

Chapter 4

1 Sroufe (1997); Lewis & Mitchell (2014); Weimer et al. (2012); Pons et al. (2004); Cutting & Dunn (1999).
2 Tsao et al. (2004); Storkel (2001).
3 Morris et al. (2007).
4 Bruner & Haste (2010); Bruner, (2013).
5 Fonagy, et al. (1991).
6 Wallace, H. M. (2003). Bruner, J. S. (2009).
7 Dahl. (2004); Blakemore & Choudhury (2006).

Chapter 5

1 Goleman (1996).
2 Schore (1994); Schore (2005).
3 Lupien et al. (2007).

Chapter 6

1 Phillips & Shonkoff (2000).

Chapter 7

1 Siegel (2012); Cozolino (2014).

Chapter 8

1 Danese & McEwen (2012); Dube et al. (2003); Felitti et al. (1998).
2 Liu & Mori (1999).
3 Valsiner (2007); Matsumoto & Juang (2012).
4 Green & Bavelier (2008); Dahlin et al. (2008).
5 Siegel (2012); Karen (1994); Gilbert (2005).
6 Cozolino (2014).
7 Feeney & Collins (2014.)

REFERENCES

Addis, D. R., Wong, A. T., & Schacter, D. L. (2007). Remembering the past and imagining the future: Common and distinct neural substrates during event construction and elaboration. *Neuropsychologia, 45*(7), 1363-1377.

Adolphs, R. (2001). The neurobiology of social cognition. *Current opinion in neurobiology, 11*(2), 231-239.

Anderson, A. K., Wais, P. E., & Gabrieli, J. D. E. (2006). Emotion enhances remembrance of neutral events past. *Proceedings of the National Academy of Sciences of the United States of America, 103*(5), 1599-1604. doi: 10.1073/pnas.0506308103.

Andreassi, J. L. (2000). *Psychophysiology: Human behavior & physiological response.* Psychology Press.

Bar, M. (2007). The proactive brain: using analogies and associations to generate predictions. *Trends in cognitive sciences, 11*(7), 280-289.

Blakemore, S. J., & Choudhury, S. (2006). Development of the adolescent brain: Implications for executive function and social cognition. *Journal of child psychology and psychiatry, 47*(3-4), 296-312.

Bradley, M. M., & Lang, P. J. (2000). Measuring emotion: Behavior, feeling, and physiology. *Cognitive neuroscience of emotion, 25*, 49-59.

REFERENCES

Bruner, J. S. (2013). Learning how to do things with words. *Psycholinguistic Research (PLE: Psycholinguistics): Implications and Applications*, 265.

Bruner, J. S. (2009). *Actual minds, possible worlds.* Harvard University Press.

Bruner, J. S., & Haste, H. (Eds.). (2010). *Making Sense (Routledge Revivals): The Child's Construction of the World.* Routledge: New York, NY.

Buckner, R. L., Andrews-Hanna, J. R., & Schacter, D. L. (2008). The brain's default network. *Annals of the New York Academy of Sciences, 1124*(1), 1-38.

Burke, A., Heuer, F., & Reisberg, D. (1992). Remembering emotional events. *Memory & Cognition, 20*(3), 277-290.

Cahill, L., Gorski, L., & Le, K. (2003). Enhanced human memory consolidation with post-learning stress: Interaction with the degree of arousal at encoding. *Learning & Memory, 10*(4), 270-274. doi: 10.1101/lm.62403.

Carter, R. (2014). *The human brain book.* DK Publishing: New York, NY.

Cozolino, L. (2014). *The neuroscience of human relationships: Attachment and the developing social brain.* WW Norton & Company.

Cutting, A. L., & Dunn, J. (1999). Theory of mind, emotion understanding, language, and family background: Individual differences and interrelations. *Child development, 70*(4), 853-865.

Danese, A., & McEwen, B. S. (2012). Adverse childhood experiences, allostasis, allostatic load, and age-related disease. *Physiology & behavior, 106*(1), 29-39.

Dahl, R. E. (2004). Adolescent brain development: A period of vulnerabilities and opportunities. Keynote address. *Annals of the New York Academy of Sciences, 1021*(1), 1-22.

Dahlin, E., Nyberg, L., Bäckman, L., & Neely, A. S. (2008). Plasticity of executive functioning in young and older adults: Immediate training gains, transfer, and long-term maintenance. *Psychology and aging, 23*(4), 720.

De Kloet, E. R., Joëls, M., & Holsboer, F. (2005). Stress and the brain: from adaptation to disease. *Nature Reviews Neuroscience, 6*(6), 463-475.

Dube, S. R., Felitti, V. J., Dong, M., Giles, W. H., & Anda, R. F. (2003). The impact of adverse childhood experiences on health problems: evidence from four birth cohorts dating back to 1900. *Preventive medicine, 37*(3), 268-277.

Feeney, B. C., & Collins, N. L. (2014). A theoretical perspective on the importance of social connections for thriving. In Mikulincer, Mario (Ed); Shaver, Phillip R. (Ed), (2014). Mechanisms of social connection: From brain to group. The Herzliya series on personality and social psychology. (pp. 291-314). Washington, DC, US: American Psychological Association, xvii, 426 pp. doi: 10.1037/14250-017

Felitti, M. D., Vincent, J., Anda, M. D., Robert, F., Nordenberg, M. D., Williamson, M. S., & James, S. (1998). Relationship of childhood abuse and household dysfunction to many of the leading causes of death in adults: The Adverse Childhood Experiences (ACE) Study. *American journal of preventive medicine, 14*(4), 245-258.

Fonagy, P., Steele, M., Steele, H., Moran, G. S., & Higgitt, A. C. (1991). The capacity for understanding mental states: The reflective self in parent and child and its significance for security of attachment. *Infant Mental Health Journal, 12*(3), 201-218.

Fuster, J (2008). *The prefrontal cortex.* Academic Press: San Diego, CA.

Gilbert, P. (2005). Social Mentalities: A Biopsychosocial and Evolutionary Approach to Social Relationships.

Goleman, D. (1996). *Vital lies, simple truths: The psychology of self deception.* Simon and Schuster.

Green, C. S., & Bavelier, D. (2008). Exercising your brain: A review of human brain plasticity and training-induced learning. *Psychology and aging, 23*(4), 692.

Gross, J. J. (1998). Antecedent-and response-focused emotion regulation: divergent consequences for experience, expression, and physiology. *Journal of personality and social psychology, 74*(1), 224.

Hamann, S. (2001). Cognitive and neural mechanisms of emotional memory. *Trends in cognitive sciences, 5*(9), 394-400.

Karen, R. (1994). *Becoming attached: First relationships and how they shape our capacity to love.* Oxford University Press.

Lewis, C., & Mitchell, P. (2014). *Children's early understanding of mind: Origins and development.* Psychology Press.

LeDoux, J.E. (2000). Emotion circuits in the brain. *Annual Reviews of Neuroscience, 23,* 155-184.

LeDoux, J. E. (2003). *Synaptic self: How our brains become who we are.* Penguin Books: New York, NY

Lillas, C. and Turnbull, J. (2009). Infant/Child Mental Health, Early Intervention, and Relationship-Based Therapies: A Neurorelational Framework for Interdisciplinary Practice. New York: Norton & Company Inc.

Liu, J., & Mori, A. (1999). Stress, aging, and brain oxidative damage. *Neurochemical research, 24*(11), 1479-1497.

Lupien, S. J., Maheu, F., Tu, M., Fiocco, A., & Schramek, T. E. (2007). The effects of stress and stress hormones on human cognition: Implications for the field of brain and cognition. *Brain and cognition, 65*(3), 209-237.

Matsumoto, D., & Juang, L. (2012). *Culture and psychology.* Cengage Learning: Belmont, CA

McEwen, B. S., & Gianaros, P. J. (2010). Central role of the brain in stress and adaptation: Links to socioeconomic status, health, and disease. *Annals of the New York Academy of Sciences, 1186*(1), 190-222.

Mitchell, J. P., Banaji, M. R., & MacRae, C. N. (2005). The link between social cognition and self-referential thought in the medial prefrontal cortex. *Journal of cognitive neuroscience, 17*(8), 1306-1315.

Morris, A. S., Silk, J. S., Steinberg, L., Myers, S. S., & Robinson, L. R. (2007). The role of the family context in the development of emotion regulation. *Social development, 16*(2), 361-388.

Perry, B. D., Pollard, R. A., Blakley, T. L., Baker, W. L., & Vigilante, D. (1995). Childhood trauma, the neurobiology of adaptation, and use dependent development of the brain: How states become traits. *Infant mental health journal, 16*(4), 271-291.

Phillips, M. L., Drevets, W. C., Rauch, S. L., & Lane, R. (2003). Neurobiology of emotion perception I: The neural basis of normal emotion perception. *Biological psychiatry, 54*(5), 504-514.

Phillips, D. A., & Shonkoff, J.P. (Eds.). (2000). *From neurons to neighborhoods: The science of early childhood development.* Washington, DC: National Academy Press

REFERENCES

Pons, F., Harris, P. L., & de Rosnay, M. (2004). Emotion comprehension between 3 and 11 years: Developmental periods and hierarchical organization. *European journal of developmental psychology*, *1*(2), 127-152.

Schacter, D. L., Addis, D. R., & Buckner, R. L. (2007). Remembering the past to imagine the future: the prospective brain. *Nature Reviews Neuroscience*, *8*(9), 657 657-661.

Schore, A. N. (1994). *Affect regulation and the origin of the self: The neurobiology of emotional development.* Psychology Press.

Schore, A. N. (2005). Back to basics attachment, affect regulation, and the developing right brain: Linking developmental neuroscience to pediatrics. *Pediatrics in Review*, *26*(6), 204-217.

Siegel, D. J. (2012). *The developing mind: How relationships and the brain interact to shape who we are.* Guilford Press.

Spencer-Oatey, H. (2008). *Culturally speaking: culture, communication and politeness theory* (pp. 258-273). Continuum International Publishing Group.

Sroufe, L. A. (1997). *Emotional development: The organization of emotional life in the early years.* Cambridge University Press.

Storkel, H. L. (2001). Learning New Words Phonotactic Probability in Language Development. *Journal of Speech, Language, and Hearing Research*, *44*(6), 1321-1337.

Tsao, F. M., Liu, H. M., & Kuhl, P. K. (2004). Speech perception in infancy predicts language development in the second year of life: a longitudinal study. *Child development*, *75*(4), 1067-1084.

Valsiner, J. (2007). Culture in minds and societies: Foundations of cultural psychology. *Psychol. Stud. (September 2009)*, *54*, 238-239.

Wallace, H. M. (2003). The reflected self: Creating yourself as (you think) others see you. *Handbook of self and identity*, 91.

Weimer, A. A., Sallquist, J., & Bolnick, R. R. (2012). Young children's emotion comprehension and theory of mind understanding. *Early Education & Development, 23*(3), 280-301.

ABOUT THE AUTHOR

Barbara Stroud is a licensed clinical psychologist who works primarily with young children and families. She has studied how early experiences influence the brain, social development, and emotional understanding, and she is passionate about improving the early relationships young children experience so that they can become healthy, happy, and socially competent adults.

An infant mental health specialist and ZERO TO THREE graduate fellow, Stroud holds a PhD in applied developmental psychology from Nova Southeastern University and has more than twenty years' experience as a trainer in the early childhood, child development, and mental health arenas. Over the years, she has presented for numerous organizations and conferences such as the American Psychological Association and Prevent Child Abuse America National Conference.

The author of several professional texts, Intentional Living is Stroud's first self-help book. Learn more about her work at DrBarbaraStroud.com.

CPSIA information can be obtained
at www.ICGtesting.com
Printed in the USA
FSHW012010050122
87442FS